CONTENTS

WELCOME UNIT 1

WELCOME!

Hello! Welcome to Tiptop English!

Mark

Angela   Boris

Count Horror

THE WELCOME SONG

Hello, Hello! and Welcome!
Welcome, everyone!
Hello, Hello and Welcome!
Welcome everyone!

UNIT ONE

LESSON ONE

FIND THE ENGLISH WORDS!

1 LOOK.

2 LISTEN AND FIND.

ice cream

bus

star

hamburger

3 DO A PUZZLE.

BAR

S	T	O	P	U	I	J	H
U	A	J	I	V	C	K	A
P	B	K	Z	W	E	L	M
E	C	L	Z	X	C	M	B
R	D	M	A	A	R	N	U
M	E	O	Q	C	E	O	R
A	T	A	X	I	A	P	G
R	F	P	R	D	M	Q	E
K	G	B	A	R	F	R	R
E	H	U	S	E	G	S	Y
T	I	S	T	S	T	A	R

SANDWICHES

ICE CREAM · DRINKS

COLD DRINKS

HOT PIZZA

COLD DRINKS · PIZZA

HAMBURGER

SNACK BAR

BUS

A

MAKE A BADGE!

1 LOOK.

GIRLS

2 LISTEN AND FIND.

4

BOYS

3 SPEAK.

Hello! I'm _____.

4 MAKE A BADGE!

I'm

· · · · · · ·

Hello! I'm Mark.

Trace

Stick

Colour

Cut

HELLO. HOW ARE YOU?

1 PLAY A GAME.

Hello, I'm _____
Hello, _____ .

Hello, I'm Janet.

Hello, Janet.

Hello, Lucy.

Hello, I'm Lucy.

Um _____

Hello, Robert.

Hello, Gail.

Hello, Anne.

Hello, Paul.

2 LISTEN. CLAP.

Hello, hello. How are you?
How are you?
I'm Boris the Cat.

4 MAKE A PUPPET.

colour

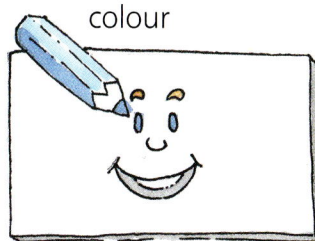

cut

glue

Hello, I'm _____.

3 SING A SONG.

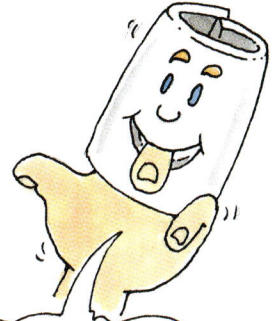

Hello!

How are you?

Hello, I'm Sammy the snake.

UNIT ONE

LESSON FOUR

COUNT HORROR'S GARDEN.

1 LOOK AND LISTEN.

2

2 ACT IT OUT.

Teacher

Mummy

Daddy

3 DO A PUZZLE. Find the words.

H	A	M	B	U	R	G	E	R	Y	S
Y	X	Y	X	Y	X	Y	X	Y	X	T
I	C	E	C	R	E	A	M	X	Y	A
X	Y	G	Y	D	A	D	D	Y	X	R
Y	X	I	X	G	A	R	D	E	N	X
B	A	R	Y	T	E	A	C	H	E	R
U	X	L	X	Y	X	Y	B	O	Y	X
S	N	A	K	E	X	M	U	M	M	Y

9

WHO IS IT?

1 LOOK AND LISTEN.

2 PLAY A GAME.

3 DO A PUZZLE.

Who is it?

It's _____ .

It's _____ .

Mark

Boris

Angela

Count Horror

It's _____ .

It's _____ .

11

MAGIC WORDS.

1 LOOK.

HELLO!

2 MAKE A MAGIC WORD.

(Fold here.)

3 PLAY A GAME.

4 WHAT'S THIS WORD?

Look!

5 DO A PUZZLE.

COUNT HORROR'S
MAGIC SOUP

Magic Word Soup

_ _ _ _ _

_ _ _

_ _ _

_ _ _ _ _

_ _ _

_ _ _ _ _

13

HELLO. COME IN. WELCOME!

1 LISTEN AND LOOK.

A castle

B garden

C door

D hall

E sitting room

2 LISTEN AND LOOK.

_____ castle

_____ house

_____ flat

3 LISTEN AND FIND.

4 REPEAT.

5 ACT IT OUT.

6 DO A PUZZLE.

7 DRAW.

My _____ .

8 LOOK AND LISTEN.

15

DRAW A HOUSE.

1 LISTEN AND DRAW.

bedroom

bathroom

kitchen

hall

garden

sitting room

16

2 READ AND FIND.

sofa

TV

chair

table

bed

fridge

bath

toilet

3 DO A PUZZLE.

KITCHEN	BEDROOM	BATHROOM	SITTING ROOM
_____	bed	_____	TV
_____	_____	_____	_____

4 PLAY A GAME.

THIS IS A TIGER.

1 LISTEN.

2 LISTEN AND FIND.   door   bus   sheep   car   tiger   cow

dog   toilet   TV   cat

FARM

STREET

18

ZOO

HOUSE

GARDEN

3 **LOOK AND FIND.**

chair   car   tiger   toilet   cow   fridge   dog   cat   table

bed   bus   sheep   TV   ice cream

BAR

RESTAURANT

19

WHAT'S THIS? IT'S A CAT.

1 COLOUR THE PICTURES.

1

DOG   CAT

CAR   STAR

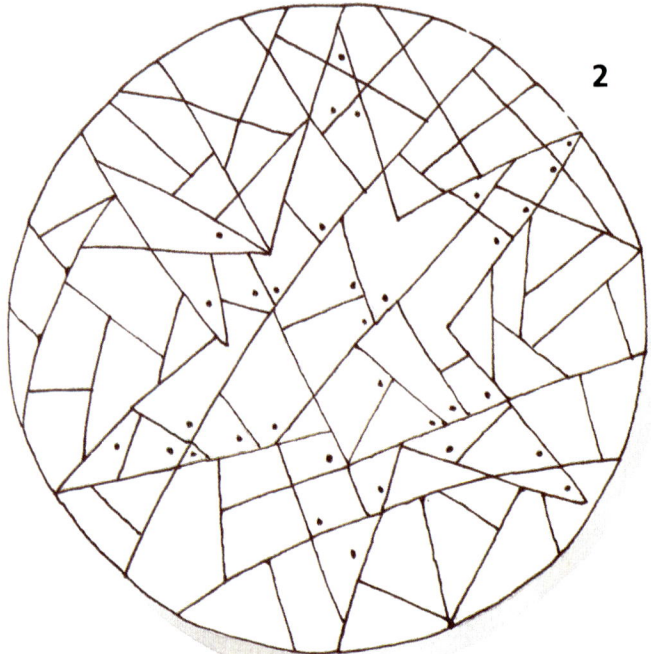

2

2 LISTEN AND FIND.

3 READ AND FIND.

3

What's this?
It's a house.
What's this?
It's a flower.
What's this?
It's a tree.

5

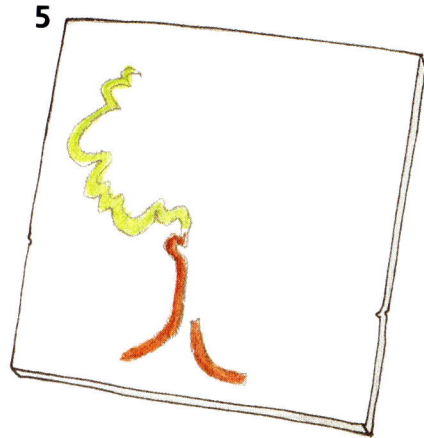

4

HOUSE

TREE   FLOWER

4 DRAW.

21

UNIT TWO

LESSON FIVE

WHAT'S THIS?

1 LISTEN AND FIND.

drum

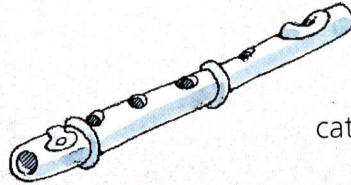
cat

dog

car

flute

clock

2 COLOUR THE PICTURE.

3 SING A SONG.

What's this ?
It's a cat.
What's this?
It's a dog.
What's this?
It's a flute.
What's this?
It's a drum.
What's this?
It's a clock.
What's this?
It's a car.

WORD GAMES.

1 PLAY A GAME. Bingo!

2 DRAW.

DO A PUZZLE.

GOOD MORNING. GOOD AFTERNOON.
IS MARK HERE? YES. / NO.

1 LISTEN AND READ.

2 LISTEN AND REPEAT.

3 PLAY A GAME.

4 LOOK AND SAY.

Is Mark here?   Is John here?   Is Patrick here?   Is Helen here?   Is Jill here?

5 LISTEN AND FIND.

GOOD EVENING.

GOOD MORNING.

GOOD AFTERNOON.

STAND UP. SIT DOWN. COME HERE. STOP. THANK YOU.

1 LOOK AND READ.

2 LISTEN AND REPEAT.

3 SPEAK.

4 **LISTEN.** The Robot Rhyme

I'm a Robot. I'm a Robot. I'm a Robot. Look at me.
I'm a Robot. I'm a Robot. I'm a Robot. Look at me.

Stand up! Come here! Go away! Turn round, and stop.
Sit down! Stand up! Turn round! Come here! Stop!

CLAP

5 **ACT IT OUT.**

6 **PLAY A GAME.**

UNIT THREE

LESSON THREE

THROW THE BALL! CATCH! HOORAY! OH DEAR!

1 LOOK AND READ.

2 SPEAK AND DO.

3 LISTEN AND FIND.

4 PLAY A GAME.

Guess the number.

5 PLAY A GAME.

one	two	three	four	five
six	seven	eight	nine	ten

6 LISTEN AND DO.

Say your name!

Draw a flower

Go away!

Sing!

Come here!

Turn round and clap

Write your name

Draw a cat

Sit down

Clap   Turn round   Say "Hello"

7 LISTEN AND FIND.

Draw a house

WHAT AM I? YOU'RE A TREE.

1 LISTEN AND FIND.

2 PLAY A GAME.
What am I?
You're a _____

LOOK AND SPEAK.

What's this?
It's a _____ .

1

2

3

What is it? Is it a bird, is it a plane?
It's Superman!

No, it isn't. It's COUNT HORROR!!

Hello, everybody!

33

MAKE A SNAKE.

1 MAKE A SNAKE.

Colour your snake.

2 MAKE A BEE.

3 LISTEN AND FIND.

4 LISTEN AND SAY.

5 DO A PUZZLE.

1,2,3,4,5,6,7,8,9,10

1 LISTEN AND SAY.

2 LISTEN AND READ.

| one | two | three | four | five | six | seven | eight | nine | ten |

3 READ AND FIND.

ten

eight

nine

one

two

three

six

four

five

seven

4 PLAY A GAME.

5 DO A PUZZLE.

one

nine

ten

two

·three

eight ·

·four

2·

·10

·9

4·

·7

3° 8

six

seven

five

·5

·6

6 WRITE.

..... stars   ..... flowers   ..... toilets   ..... balls

UNIT FOUR

LESSON ONE

COLOURS.

1 LOOK.

white

black

red

yellow

green

blue

2 LISTEN AND FIND.

3 DRAW.

a black cat

a red flower

a blue ball

4 COLOUR THE PICTURE.

r = red   b = blue   y = yellow   g = green

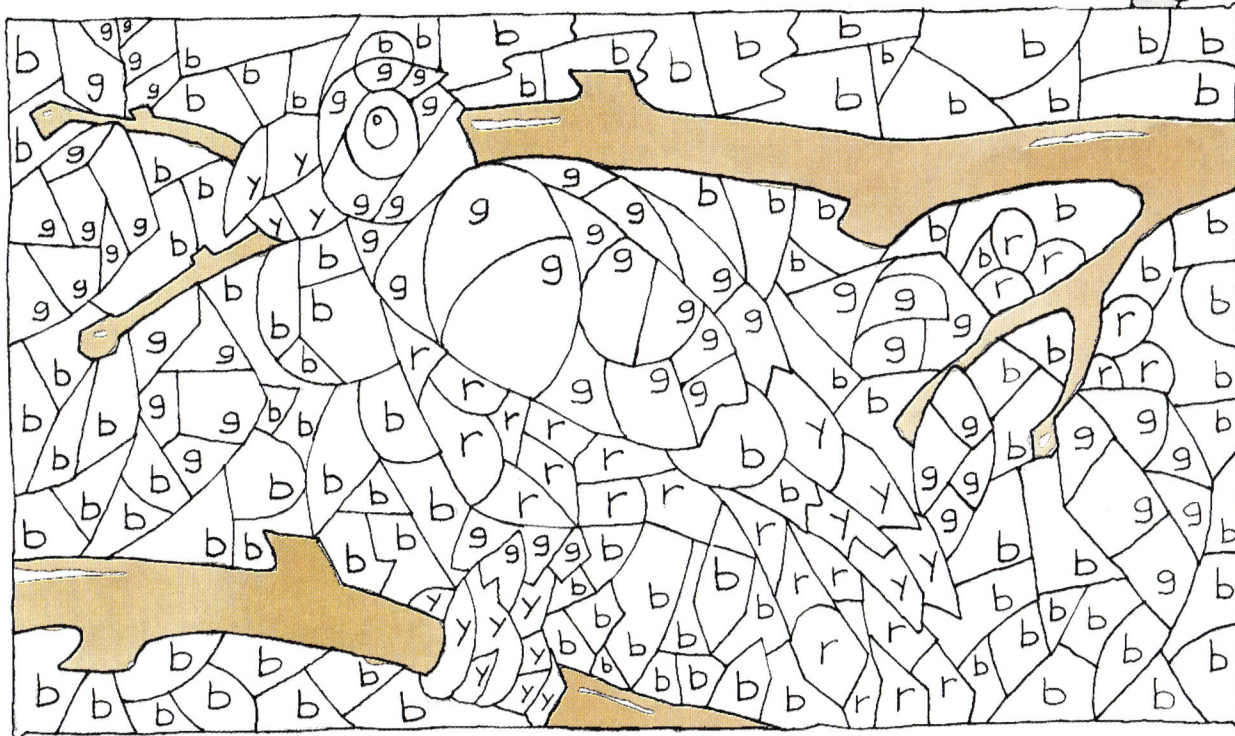

5 LISTEN.

The Green Trees Rhyme

Green trees. Green trees.
Everywhere green trees.

Blue sky. Green trees.
Everywhere green trees.

Yellow flowers. Green trees.
Everywhere green trees.

6 CLAP.

7 SAY THE RHYME.

RED AND YELLOW MAKE ORANGE.

1 COLOUR THE PICTURES.

red and yellow   make orange

yellow and blue   make green

blue and red   make purple

Black and white   make grey

white and red   make pink

2 LISTEN.

3 MAKE NEW COLOURS.

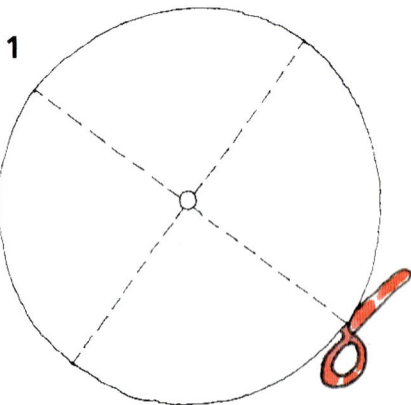

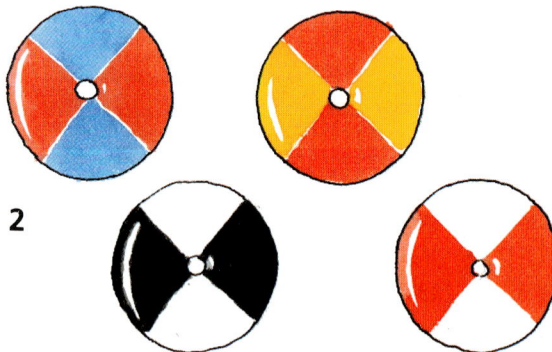

1

2

3

4 READ AND FIND.

BLUE PINK ORANGE BROWN RED WHITE BLACK GREEN YELLOW PURPLE

5 SPEAK.

What is your favourite colour?

My favourite colour is BLACK!

6 COLOUR THE RAINBOW.

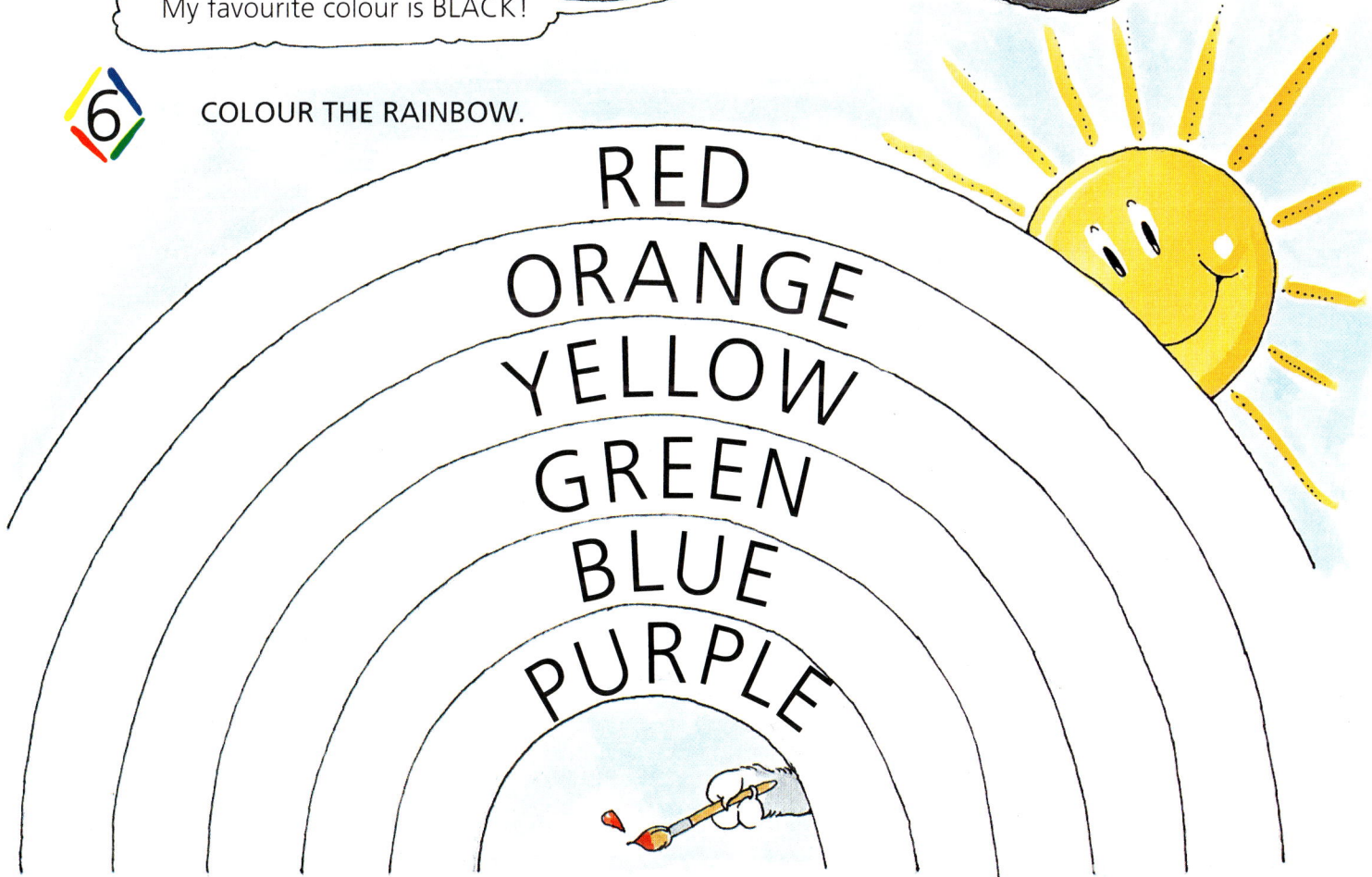

RED
ORANGE
YELLOW
GREEN
BLUE
PURPLE

HOW MANY DOGS CAN YOU SEE?

1 LISTEN AND FIND.

1

2

3

4

2 LISTEN AND REPEAT.

3 WRITE.

I can see _____ stars.

I can _____ five _____ .

42

4 LISTEN AND LOOK.
The Tree Rhyme

One two three, I can see
Four cats in this tree.

One two three, I can see
Five snakes in this tree.

One two three, I can see
Six tigers in this tree.

One two three, I can see
Eight bees in this tree.

Oh dear! It's falling down!

5 SPEAK.

Say the rhyme.

6 MAKE A TREE.

1 green

brown

Colour

2 Roll

3 Cut

4 Pull

43

UNIT FOUR

LESSON FOUR

ON THE FARM.

1 LISTEN AND FIND.

cow

cat

dog

duck

pig

horse

turkey

chicken

2 SING THE SONG.

3 DO A PUZZLE.

How many pigs can you see?
How many cows?
How many dogs?
How many cats?
How many turkeys?
How many ducks?
How many chickens?
How many horses?

4 SPEAK.

I can see three cats

44

⑤ LOOK AND FIND.

pig
horse
chicken
turkey
cat
cow
dog
duck

Animals   Birds

How many animals can you see? How many birds?

45

MR MACDONALD'S FARM.

1 LISTEN.

2 LOOK AND FIND THE WORDS.

a farm   some grapes   some potatoes   some carrots   some pears

3 LOOK AND FIND.

Fruit

carrots

pears

lemons

Vegetables

grapes

potatoes

cabbages

4 PLAY A GAME.

some cows   a duck   three turkeys   some ducks   some lemons   a cabbage

47

OLD MACDONALD HAS A FARM.

1 **LOOK AND SAY.**

What can you see in the picture?
I can see some pigs.
I can see some _____ .
Listen. What's this?

2 **SING A SONG.**

Listen.
Old Macdonald has
a farm,
EIEIO
And on this farm he
has some pigs. . .

SING.

chickens
ducks
turkeys
dogs
cats
horses

4 COLOUR THE PICTURE.

5 WRITE.

Old Macdonald has a farm, and on this farm he has

some _____ and

some _____ and

some _____ and

some _____ and

some _____ and

some _____ and

some _____

What a terrible noise!

49

CAN I HAVE SOME APPLES, PLEASE?

1 LISTEN AND FIND.

ZOO SHOP

Bananas for
the
monkeys

Apples for
the
horses

Carrots and tomatoes
for the rabbits

Potatoes for
the
llamas

Food for the animals

2 LISTEN AND REPEAT.

3 ACT IT OUT.

Hello, can I have some bananas, please?
Yes, of course. How many?
Six, please.
Here you are.
Thank you very much. Goodbye.

PLAY A GAME.

DO A PUZZLE.   Find the words.

A	I	B	J	W	X	J	K	V	P	W	H	I	V	C	W	K
P	E	A	R	S	Y	L	E	M	O	N	S	J	U	A	X	J
P	H	N	K	T	Z	I	L	U	T	X	G	K	T	R	Y	I
L	G	A	L	S	A	H	M	T	A	Y	F	L	S	R	Z	H
E	F	N	M	R	B	G	N	S	T	O	M	A	T	O	E	S
S	E	A	N	O	C	F	O	R	O	Z	E	M	R	T	A	G
A	D	S	O	P	D	E	P	Q	E	A	D	N	Q	S	B	F
B	C	C	A	B	B	A	G	E	S	B	C	O	P	C	D	E

LOOK AND FIND.

51

LESSON TWO

WHAT'S FOR DINNER?

1 LOOK AND FIND.

salad

onions

biscuits

soup

cabbage

rice

steak

apple pie

fish

broccoli

beans

chips

ice cream

carrots

2 LISTEN AND FIND.

3 **LISTEN AND REPEAT.**

4 **ACT IT OUT.**

What's for dinner?
_____
Mm! Lovely!
Ugh! Horrible!

5 **DO A PUZZLE.**

POSU
° ° °

KETAS NAD PICHS

LADSA
° ° °

LEPPA EPI

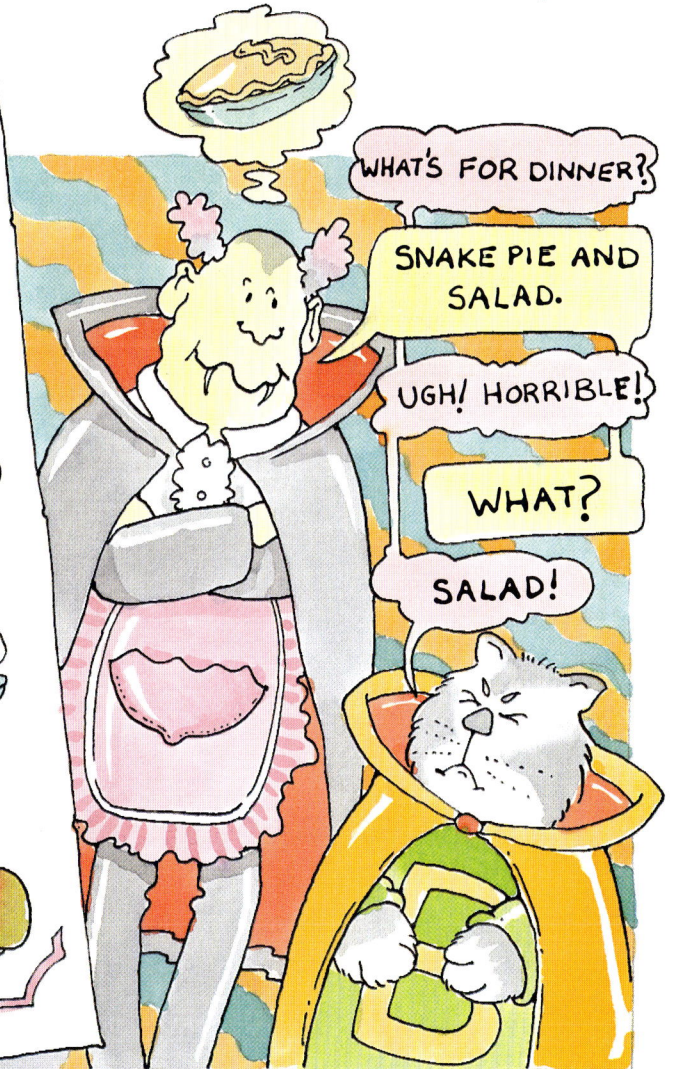

WHAT'S FOR DINNER?

SNAKE PIE AND SALAD.

UGH! HORRIBLE!

WHAT?

SALAD!

53

UNIT FIVE

LESSON THREE

I LIKE ICE CREAM.

1 LISTEN AND FIND.

2 PLAY A GAME.

3 LISTEN AND FIND.

I like

I don't like

4 LISTEN AND REPEAT.

5 LOOK AND FIND.

Lovely! I like ice cream.

Lovely! I like fish.

Grr. I like meat.

Horrible! I don't like chicken.

Mm! I like carrots.

Lovely! I like grapes.

6 SPEAK.

7 ACT IT OUT.

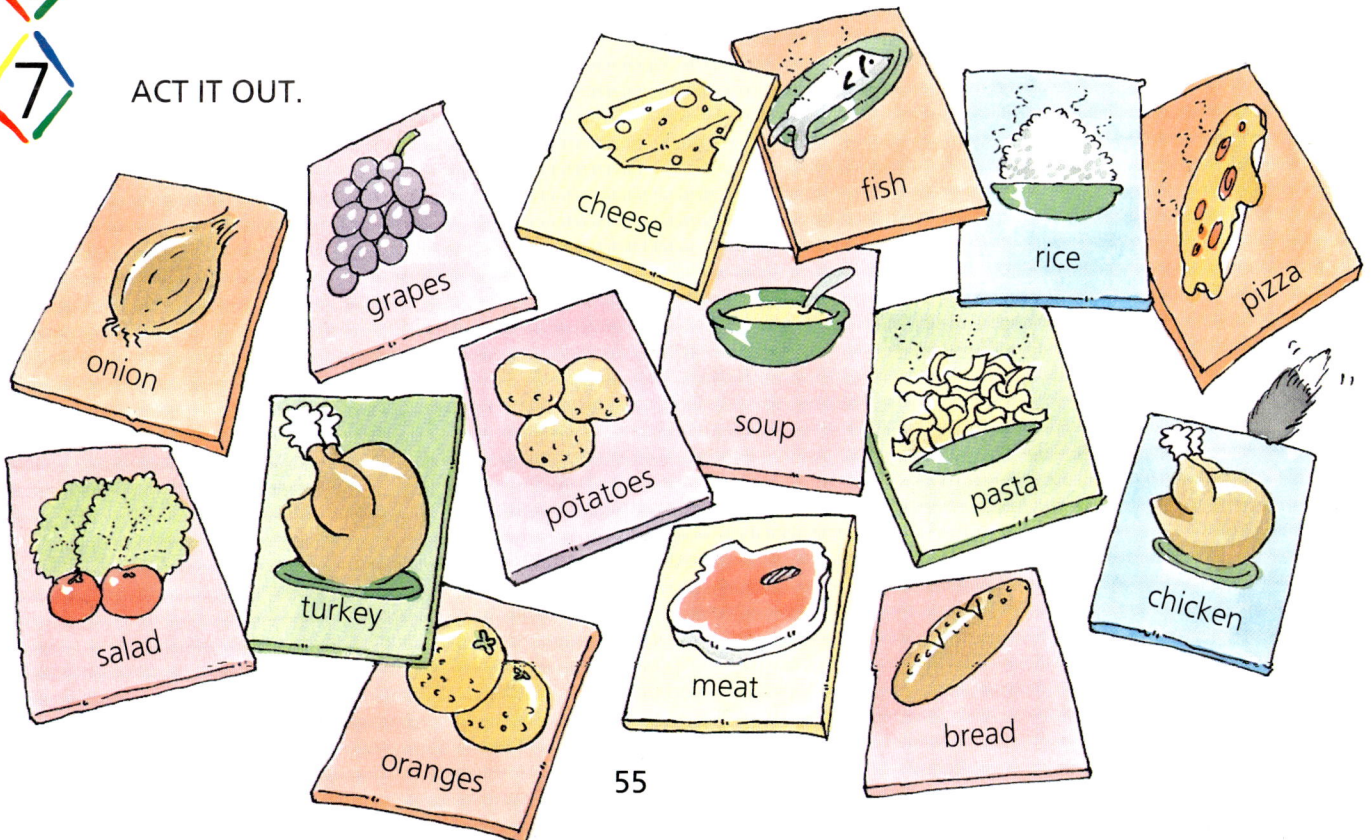

cheese

fish

rice

pizza

grapes

onion

soup

pasta

potatoes

salad

turkey

meat

chicken

bread

oranges

55

UNIT FIVE

LESSON FOUR

THIS IS AN APPLE.

1 LISTEN AND FIND.

2 LISTEN AND WRITE.

A

A c _____

A d _____

A h _____

A l _____

A t _____

An _____

An elephant

An _____

An _____

An umbrella

An

56

THINK.

'A' or 'An'?

4 DO A PUZZLE.

What can you see in the picture? Write the words.

_____ _____ _____

_____ _____ _____

_____

5 SPEAK.

I can see an _____

a _____

UNIT FIVE

LESSON FIVE

I'M HUNGRY.

1 LISTEN AND FIND.

2 LISTEN AND REPEAT.

3 READ AND FIND.

some water

some milk

some bread

some lemonade

an apple

some cheese

an orange

a banana

4 LOOK AND FIND.

HUNGRY OR THIRSTY?

1

2

3

5

4

6

5 LISTEN.

6 PLAY A GAME.

59

THE HUNGRY ELEPHANT.

1 LISTEN AND FIND.

some bread

an apple

some cheese

some potatoes

an orange

a pear

some onions

2 LISTEN AND SPEAK.

3 PLAY A GAME.

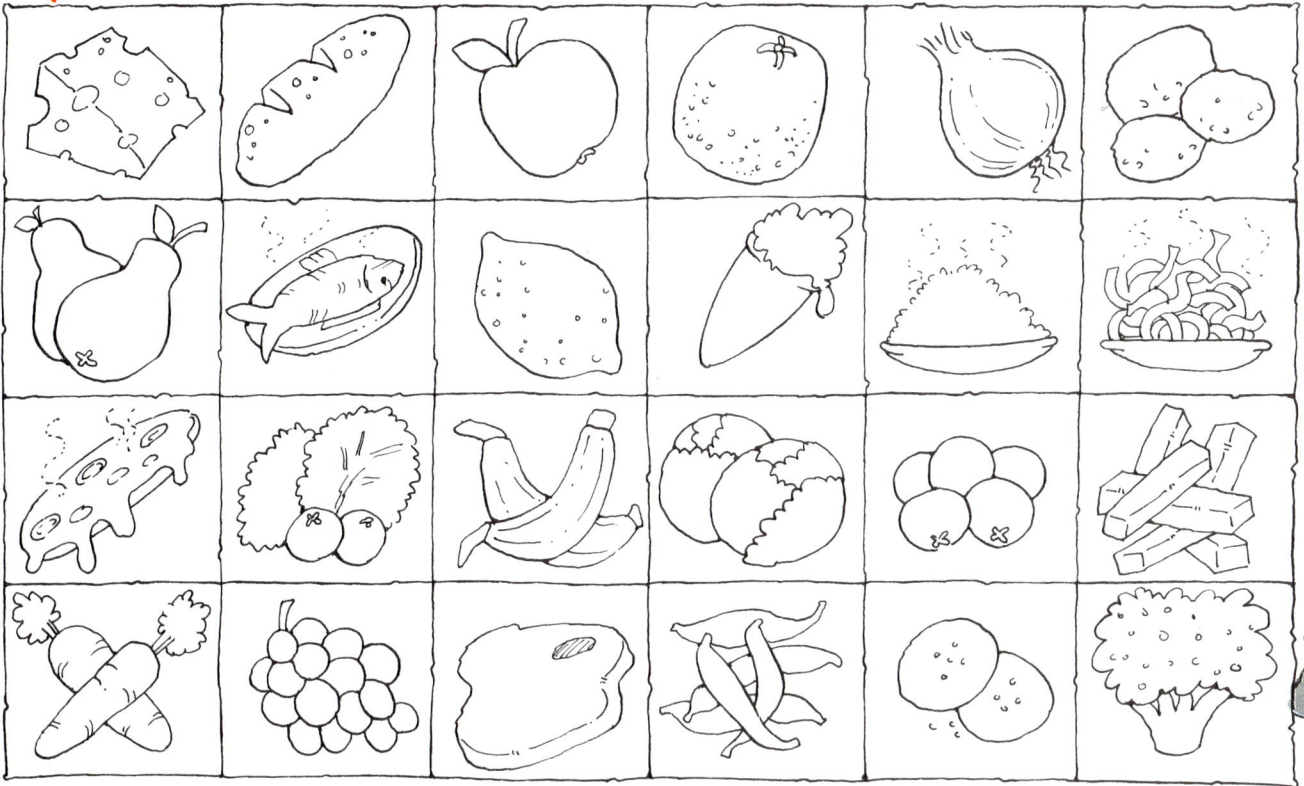

4 COLOUR THE PICTURES.

5 DRAW.

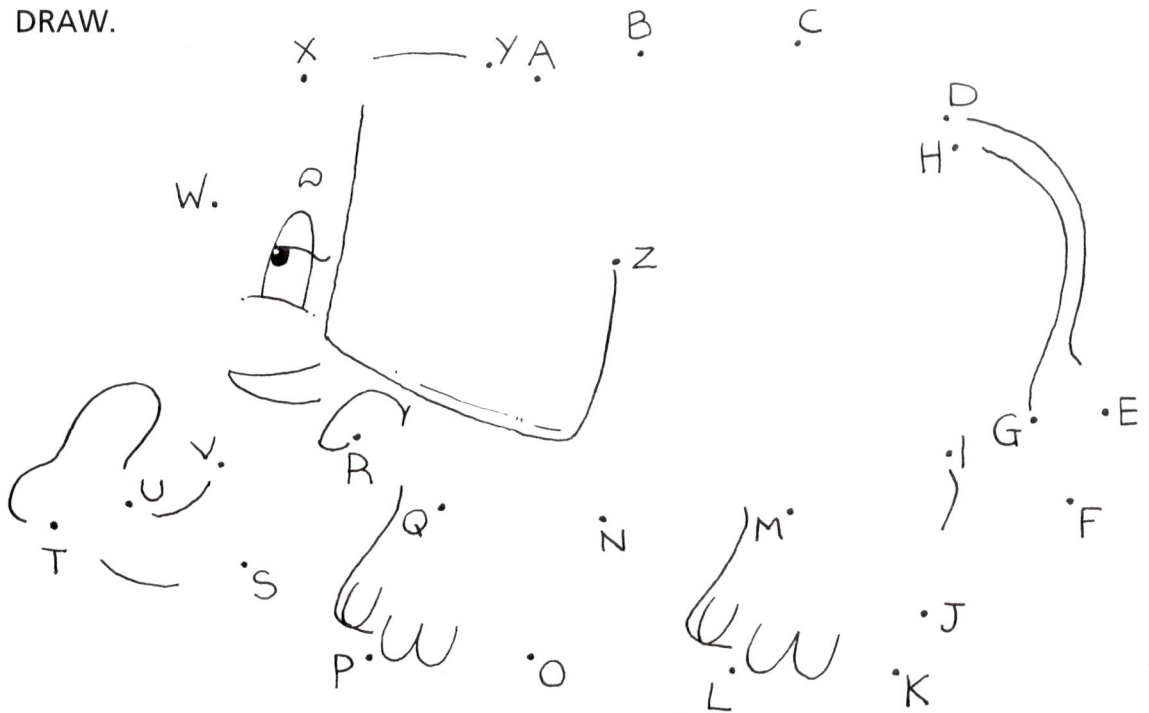

THE ALPHABET

1 LOOK AND LISTEN.

ABCDEFGHIJKLM

a b c d e f g h i j k l m

NOPQRSTUVWXYZ

n o p q r s t u v w x y z

2 LOOK.

Jj Kk Ww Xx Yy

3 WRITE.

John _____

Kitchen _____

White _____

Six _____

Yellow _____

4 LISTEN AND REPEAT.

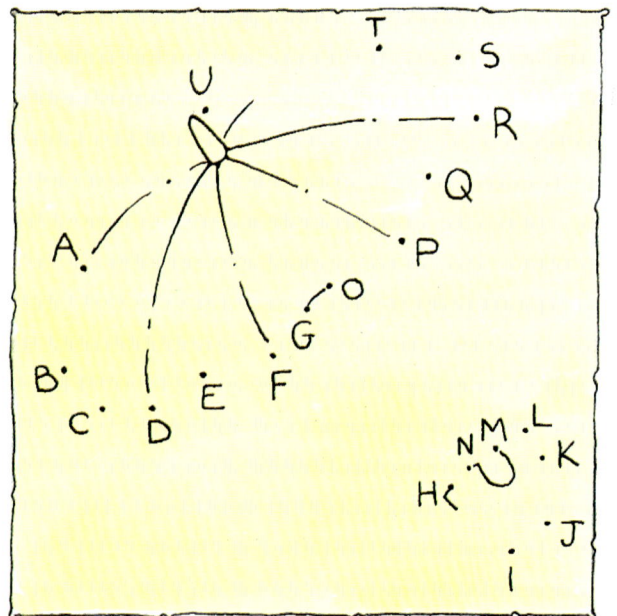

5 READ AND DRAW.

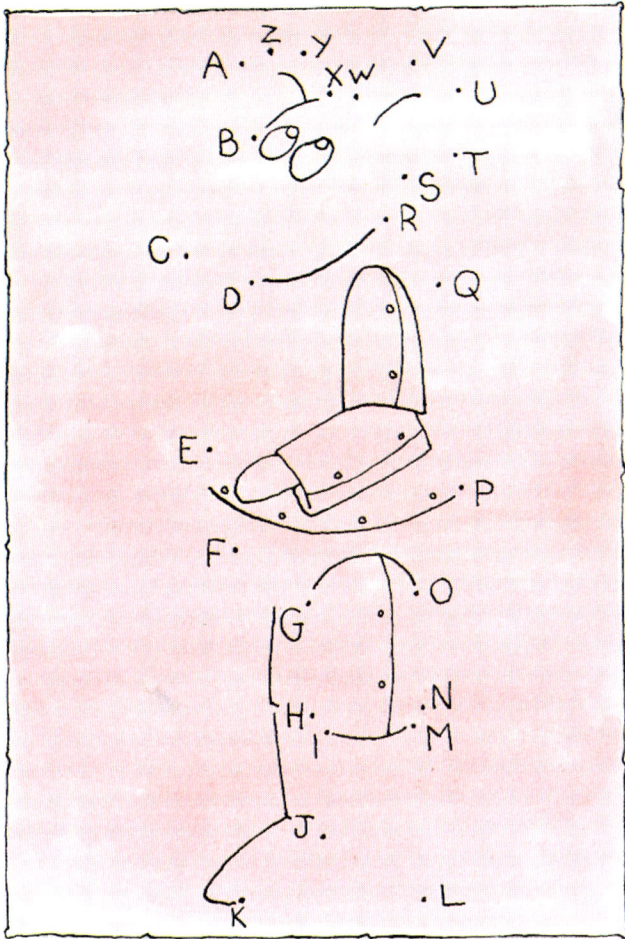

1 This is a _____

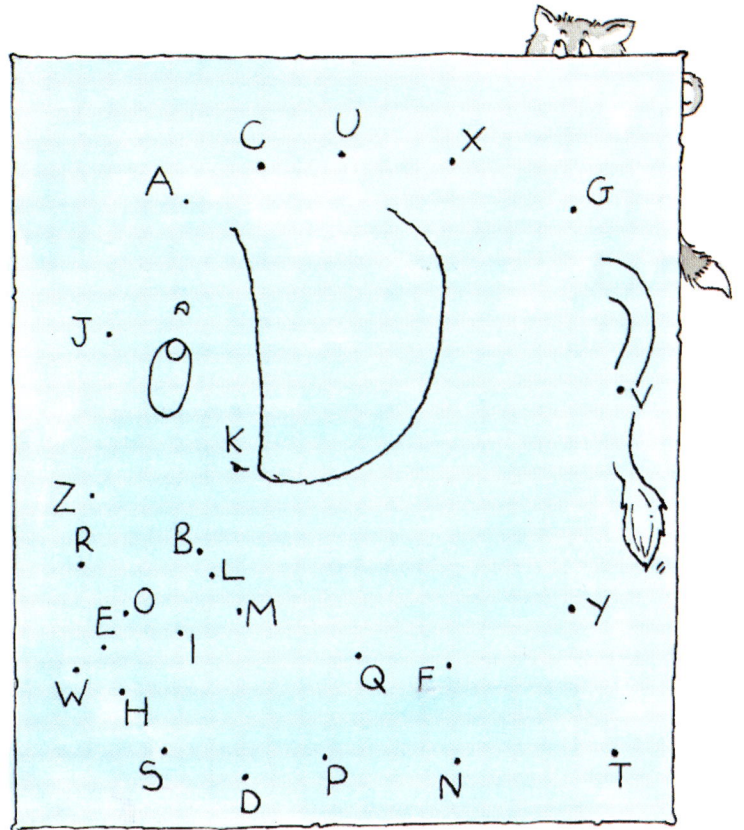

2 This is an _____

RDBI

OBY

IXS

LRIG

LUMBLEAR

PANELETH

CAN YOU SPELL YOUR NAME?

1 LISTEN AND FIND.

ANGELA   JANET   JOHN   CHRISTOPHER   PATRICK

2 SPEAK.   Say the alphabet.

A B C D E F G H I J K L M N O P Q R S T U V W X Y Z

3 SPEAK.   Can you spell your name?

4 PLAY A GAME.

ABC, I can see
Something beginning with D.

What is it? What is it?
Is it a door? No!
Is it a dog? Yes!

PLAY A GAME.

Bingo!

A	B	C	D	E	F

G	H	I	K	L	M
		jumper			

J

N	O	P	Q	R	S
nut			queen		

T	U	V	W	Y	Z
		violin	x-ray	yacht	zebra

X

65

WHAT COLOUR ARE YOUR EYES?

1 LISTEN AND FIND.

2 ACT IT OUT.

Miaow! My eyes are green. You're a cat. Yes.
Aah! My eyes are purple. You're Count Horror. Yes.

3 PROJECT.

What colour are your eyes? brown? grey? blue? green? black?

Write.

In my class _____ students have grey eyes.

_____ students have _____ eyes.

_____ students _____ brown eyes.

_____ _____ have green _____

_____ _____ have _____ eyes.

4 MAKE A CHART.

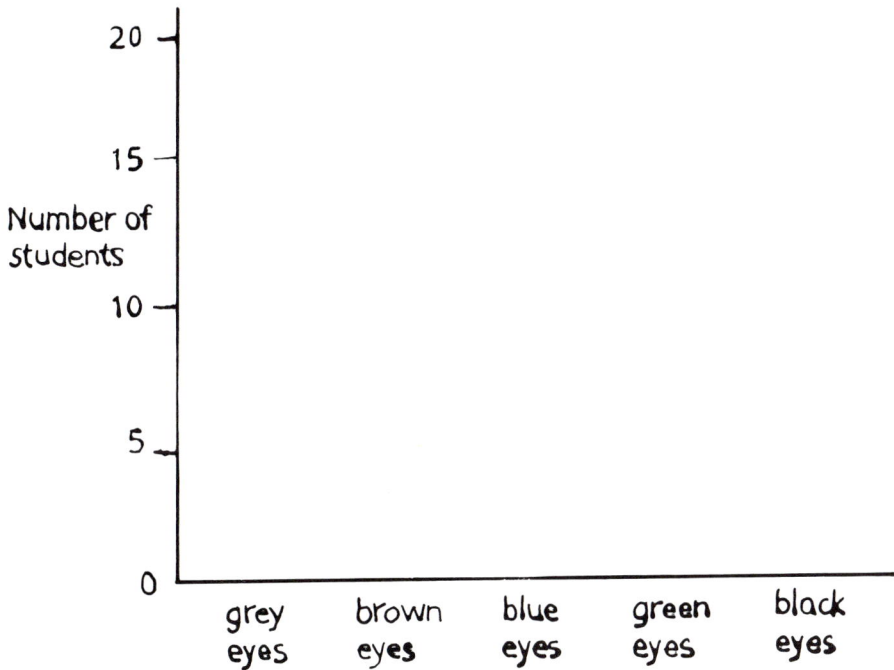

Number of students

20
15
10
5
0

grey eyes | brown eyes | blue eyes | green eyes | black eyes

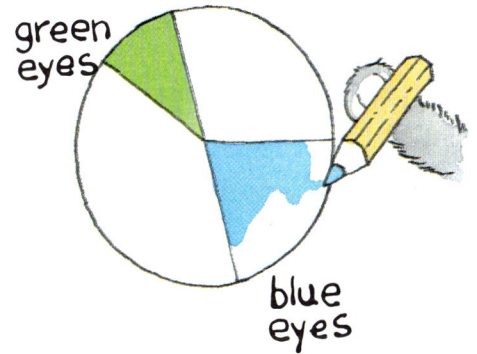

green eyes

blue eyes

5 LISTEN AND LOOK.

6 SPEAK.   Say the rhyme.

THE EYES RHYME
Some people have blue eyes. Some people have grey eyes.
Some people have brown and some have green.
Some people have black eyes, but all eyes are beautiful if they are kind.
All eyes are beautiful if they are kind.

LESSON FOUR

MAKE A MASK.

1 LISTEN AND LOOK.

UGH!

2 MAKE A COUNT HORROR MASK.

1 Copy the picture.

2 Colour his face green!

3 Cut out his eyes. Cut out his mouth.

4 Cut out his nose and fold it.

5 Cut out the mask. Remember his ears!

6 Make some hair. Use wool or paper.

7 Stick the hair on.

8 GLUE. Make some yellow teeth.

9 Stick them on!

10 Make two holes in his ears and put in some elastic.

NOW YOU ARE COUNT HORROR! SAY 'HA! HA! HA!

Now copy Boris the Cat and make a mask.

③ ACT IT OUT.

Hello, Boris. How are you?

Very well, thank you. How are you?

④ LOOK AND FIND.

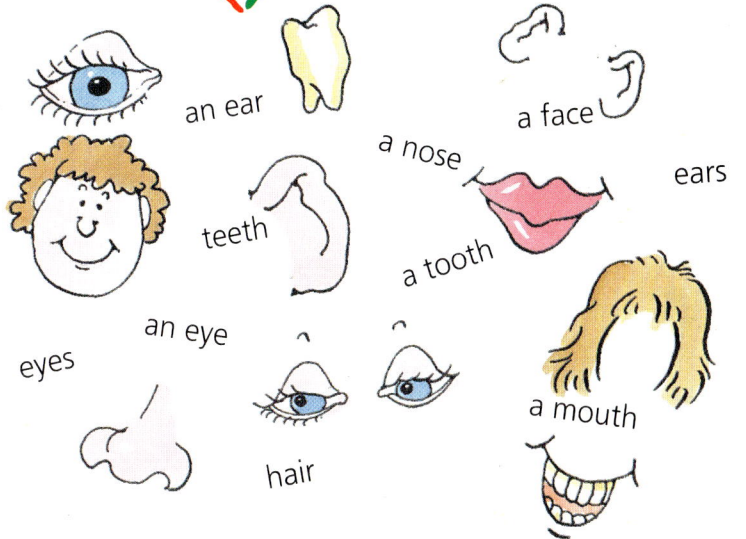

an ear

a face

a nose

ears

teeth

a tooth

an eye

eyes

a mouth

hair

COUNT HORROR'S MAGIC WORD SOUP.

1 LISTEN AND LOOK.

2 LISTEN AND REPEAT.

DO A PUZZLE.

How many words can you find in Count Horror's Magic Soup?

A	L	W	C	J	R	B	J	N	U	M	B	E	R	V
B	M	X	P	O	T	A	T	O	B	N	Y	F	K	W
C	N	Y	E	K	S	C	R	P	B	Q	Z	G	L	X
D	P	C	A	T	T	D	E	L	E	P	H	A	N	T
E	C	A	R	L	U	E	D	Q	E	R	O	I	M	Y
F	Q	B	D	M	V	F	K	R	B	D	R	U	M	Z
G	R	B	O	Y	W	G	L	S	C	T	S	J	P	A
H	S	A	E	E	X	A	X	T	E	Y	E	S	Q	B
D	O	G	F	S	O	N	G	U	D	U	A	N	R	C
I	T	E	G	N	Y	D	O	V	F	V	B	A	S	D
J	U	A	H	P	Z	H	M	W	G	W	C	K	T	E
K	V	B	I	Q	A	I	O	X	H	X	D	E	U	F

SPEAK. Tell the class your words.
'D O G, Dog'

PLAY A GAME.

71

I AM TALL.

1 LISTEN AND FIND.

2 READ AND FIND.

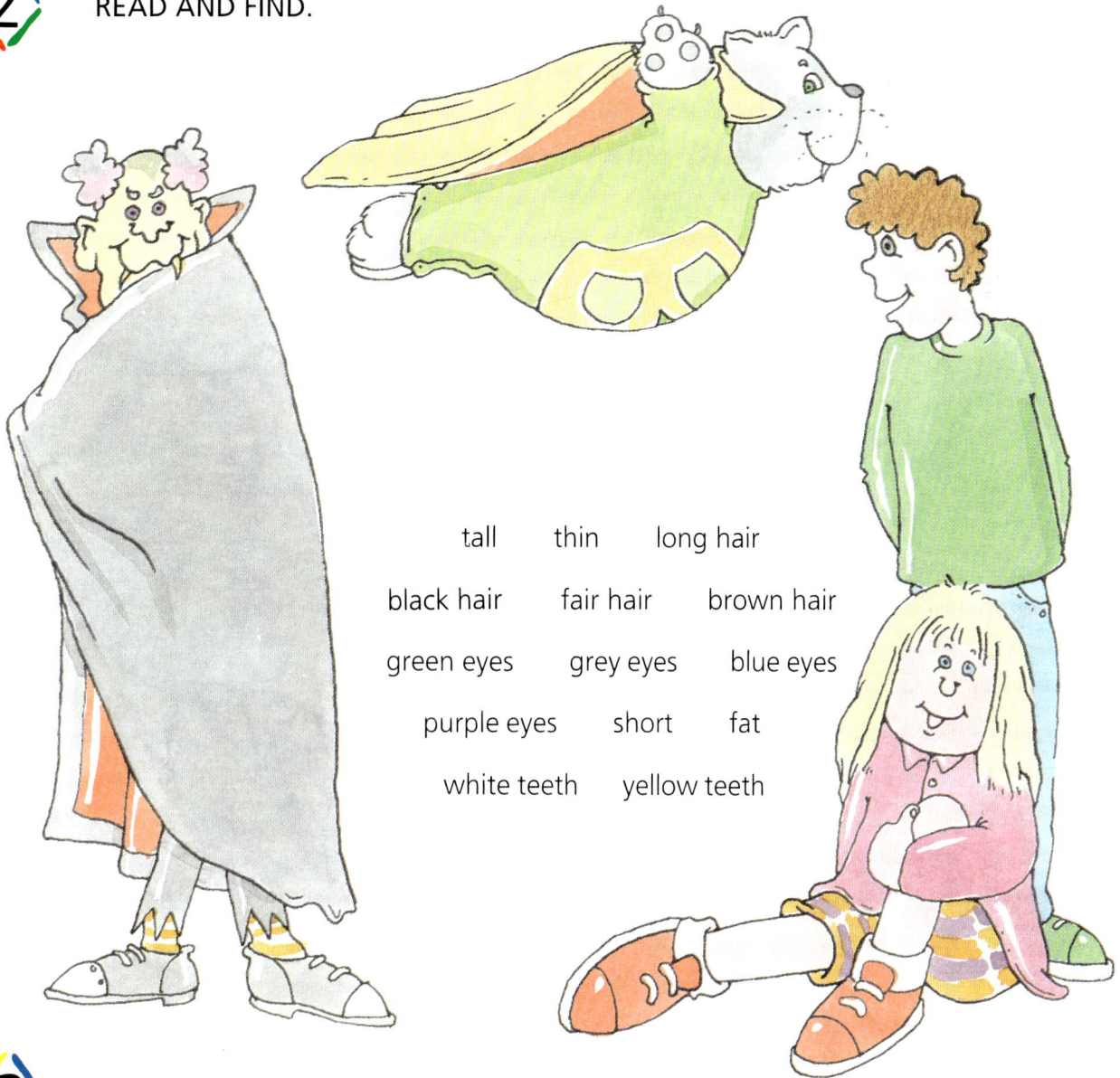

tall　　thin　　long hair

black hair　　fair hair　　brown hair

green eyes　　grey eyes　　blue eyes

purple eyes　　short　　fat

white teeth　　yellow teeth

3 PLAY A GAME. Who is it?

MY FRIENDS

1 **LISTEN.**

2 **SING THE SONG.**

I like you and you like me.
We are friends.
We are friends, we are friends.
It's good to have a friend.

3 **THINK AND WRITE.**

My friend is a boy/girl.
He/she has short/long
black/fair/brown hair and
blue/green/grey/brown/black eyes.

He/she is tall/not very tall/short.
He/she likes
ice cream/animals/cars/fruit/.....
Who is your friend?
What has your friend got on today?

4 **LOOK AND DRAW.**

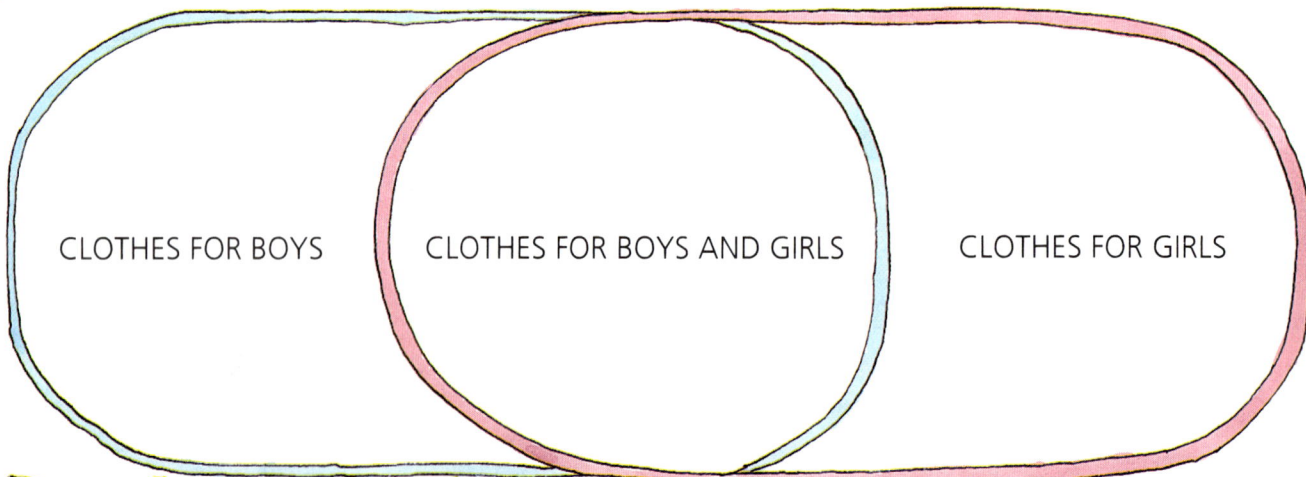

CLOTHES FOR BOYS   CLOTHES FOR BOYS AND GIRLS   CLOTHES FOR GIRLS

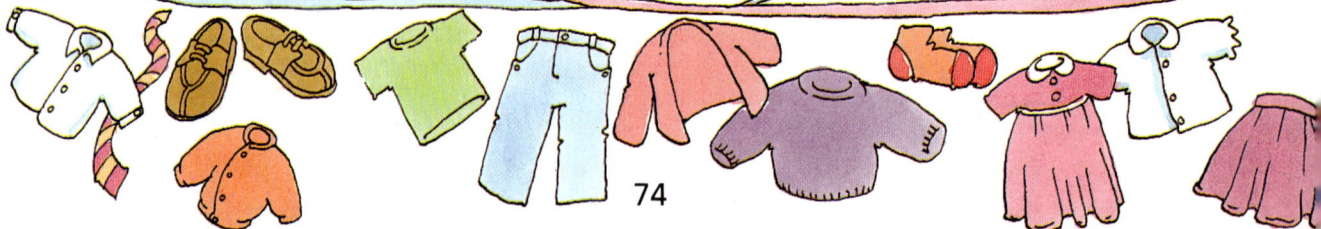

5 READ AND FIND.

Mark's shirt is blue.
Angela's blouse is yellow.
Janet's dress is green and white.
Angela's skirt is black and yellow.
Mark's jumper is grey.
Mark's trousers are blue.
Mark's shoes are black.
Angela's shoes are white.
Mark's socks are green.

Mark Janet Angela

6 SPEAK.

7 LOOK AND FIND.

Janet's jumper is green.

Angela's T-shirt is black.

Mark's tie is red.

skirt

dress

blouse

jumper

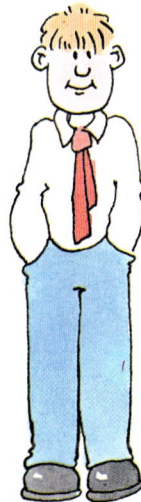  

T-shirt

tie

socks

shirt

trousers

8 SPEAK.

Describe your friend.

My friend is a girl.
She has brown hair.

LESSON TWO

THIS IS MARK'S PEN. THIS IS ANGELA'S BOOK.

1 LISTEN AND FIND.

2 PLAY A GAME.

This is Paul's pen!

No, it isn't!

3 DO A PUZZLE.

EPNLIC

NIKEF

BURBRE

MOCIC

BOKO

LURER

GAB

NEP

THIS IS MISS BLACK. THIS IS HER DESK.

1 LISTEN AND FIND.

window

Mark's class

CLASS 4B

desk

cupboard

2 THINK.

This is Mr Brown.   This is his desk.
This is Miss Black.   This is her desk.

3 PLAY A GAME.

Show me the cupboard.
Show me Laura's bag.

4 MAKE NOTICES.

This is Miss Black's desk.

This is the door.

DON'T BE SILLY!

1 LISTEN AND LOOK.

2 LOOK AND DRAW.

Don't be silly!

It's horrible!

Be careful!

Please don't sing.

Don't be afraid!

Come out at once!

Be quiet!

3 ACT IT OUT.

4 PLAY A GAME.

One, two three,
I can see something red and black.

Is it Mark's T-shirt?

Yes/No.

I CAN'T FIND MY BAG.

1 LISTEN AND FIND.

☐ soup pot ☐ sitting room ☐ kitchen ☐ bathroom ☐ fridge ☐ cupboard
☐ chair ☐ table ☐ sink

2 SPEAK.

3 PLAY A GAME.

What's on the table?

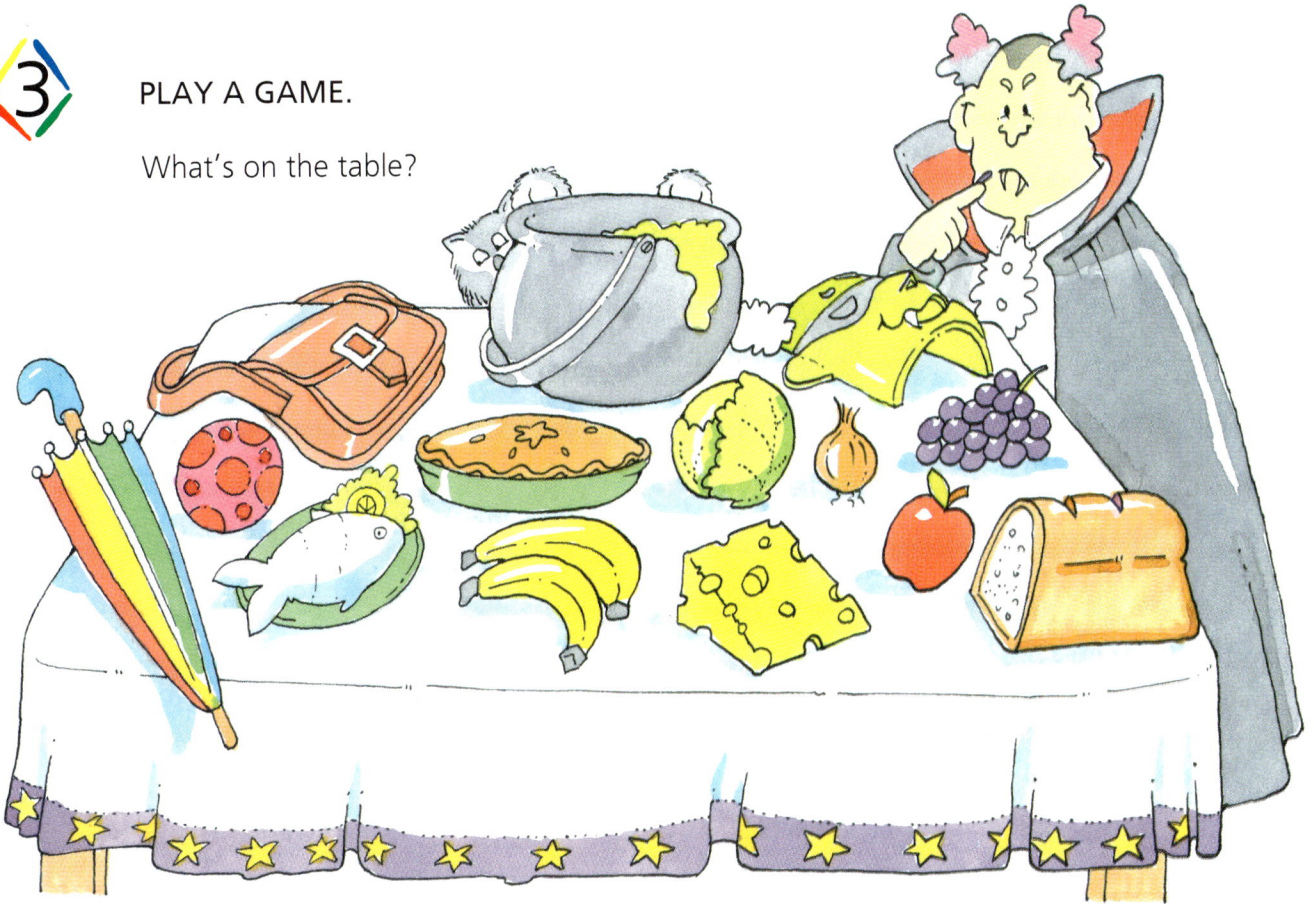

4 DO A PUZZLE.   What's in the bag?

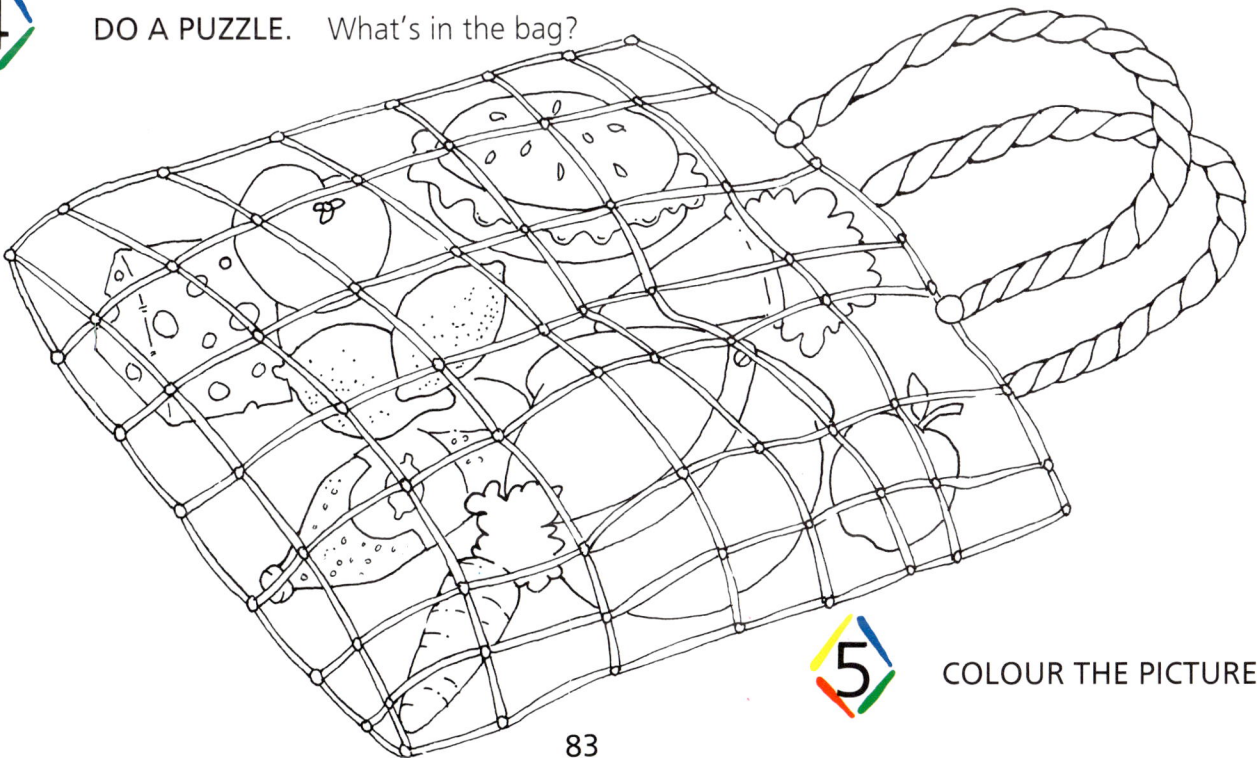

5 COLOUR THE PICTURE

83

THE TREE IN THE WOOD

1 **LISTEN AND FIND.**

2 **SING THE SONG.**

1 In a wood there is a tree
A lovely tree as you can see.

The tree is in the wood
And the green leaves grow around
  around around
And the green leaves grow around.

2 And on this tree there is a branch
A lovely branch as you can see.

The tree is in the wood
The branch is on the tree
And the green leaves grow around
  around around
And the green leaves grow around.

3 And on this branch there is a nest
A lovely nest as you can see.

The nest is on the branch
The branch is on the tree
The tree is in the wood
And the green leaves grow around
  around around
And the green leaves grow around.

4 And in this nest there is an egg
A lovely egg as you can see.

The egg is in the nest
The nest is on the branch
The branch is on the tree
The tree is in the wood
And the green leaves grow around
  around around
And the green leaves grow around.

5 And in this egg there is a bird
A lovely bird as you can see.

The bird is in the egg
The egg is in the nest
The nest is on the branch
The branch is on the tree
The tree is in the wood
And the green leaves grow around
  around around
And the green leaves grow around.

84

COLOUR THE PICTURES.

WRITE.

tree   wood   branch   nest   egg   bird

85

MARK'S HOUSE IS IN LONDON.

1 LISTEN AND FIND.

2 READ AND FIND.

Mark is English. He is from England.
Franz is German. He is from Germany.
Pilar is Spanish. She is from Spain.
Pierre is French. He is from France.
Rulla is Greek. She is from Greece.
Anna is Italian. She is from Italy.
Heidi is Swiss. She is from Switzerland.
Maria is Portuguese. She is from Portugal.

3 PROJECT.

Where are you from?

4 PLAY A GAME.

VAMPIRES COME FROM TRANSYLVANIA

1 LISTEN AND FIND.

2 WRITE.

Princess Horror
(mother)

COUNT HORROR

lives in _____ .

Storm (brother)

Sanguina (sister)

Prince Horror
(father)

HIS BROTHER AND SISTER

live in _____ .

3 WRITE.

4 READ AND FIND.

PANDAS

VAMPIRES

KANGAROOS

TIGERS

ZEBRAS

ELEPHANTS

What do you know?

Vampires come from _____

Tigers come from _____

Elephants come from _____ and_____

Zebras come from _____

Kangaroos come from _____

Pandas come from _____

5 LISTEN AND REPEAT.

THERE'S SOMETHING IN THE CUPBOARD.

1 LISTEN AND FIND.

2 READ AND FIND.

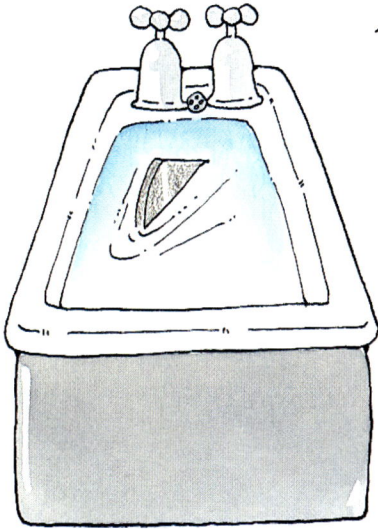

There's something on the cupboard.

There's something in the cupboard.

There's something under my bed.

There's something in the bath.

3 PLAY A GAME.

4 DO A PUZZLE.

There's something in the tree.
What is it?
It's a _____.

5 COLOUR THE PICTURE.

UNIT EIGHT

LESSON FOUR

HE CAN FLY, SHE CAN SWIM.

1 LISTEN, READ AND LOOK.

He can fly.

She can swim.

He can dance.

They can't dance.

She can't skate.

He can't play
the violin.

2 LISTEN AND FIND.

Hello.

3 SPEAK.   Can you ...? Say   Yes, I can./ No, I can't.

Quiz   What do you know about animals?

Can tigers swim?
Can penguins fly?
Can penguins swim?
Can ducks fly?
Can snakes swim?
Can elephants sit down?

Yes, they can.
No, they can't.

4 SING A SONG.

I'm a vampire, I'm a vampire. I can fly!
I can fly, but I can't cry!
Vampires can't cry.
Oh why can't I cry?
It's absurd. It's absurd.
I can't cry.

I'm a boy, I'm a boy, I can't fly.
I can cry, but I can't fly!
Oh why can't I fly?

I'm a penguin. I'm a bird.
Birds can fly, but I can't fly.
Penguins can't fly.
Oh why can't I fly?
It's absurd. I'm a bird.
But I can't fly!

93

I LIKE THE BLUE ONE.

1 LISTEN AND FIND.

2 WRITE.

Write the words on the T-shirts.
Write your name on the green one.

I ♥ ICE CREAM.   HELLO! I'M _____.   I LOVE TREES.   I LIKE COUNT HORROR.

SPEAK.

Which T-shirt do you like?
The blue one.

4 **DRAW.**

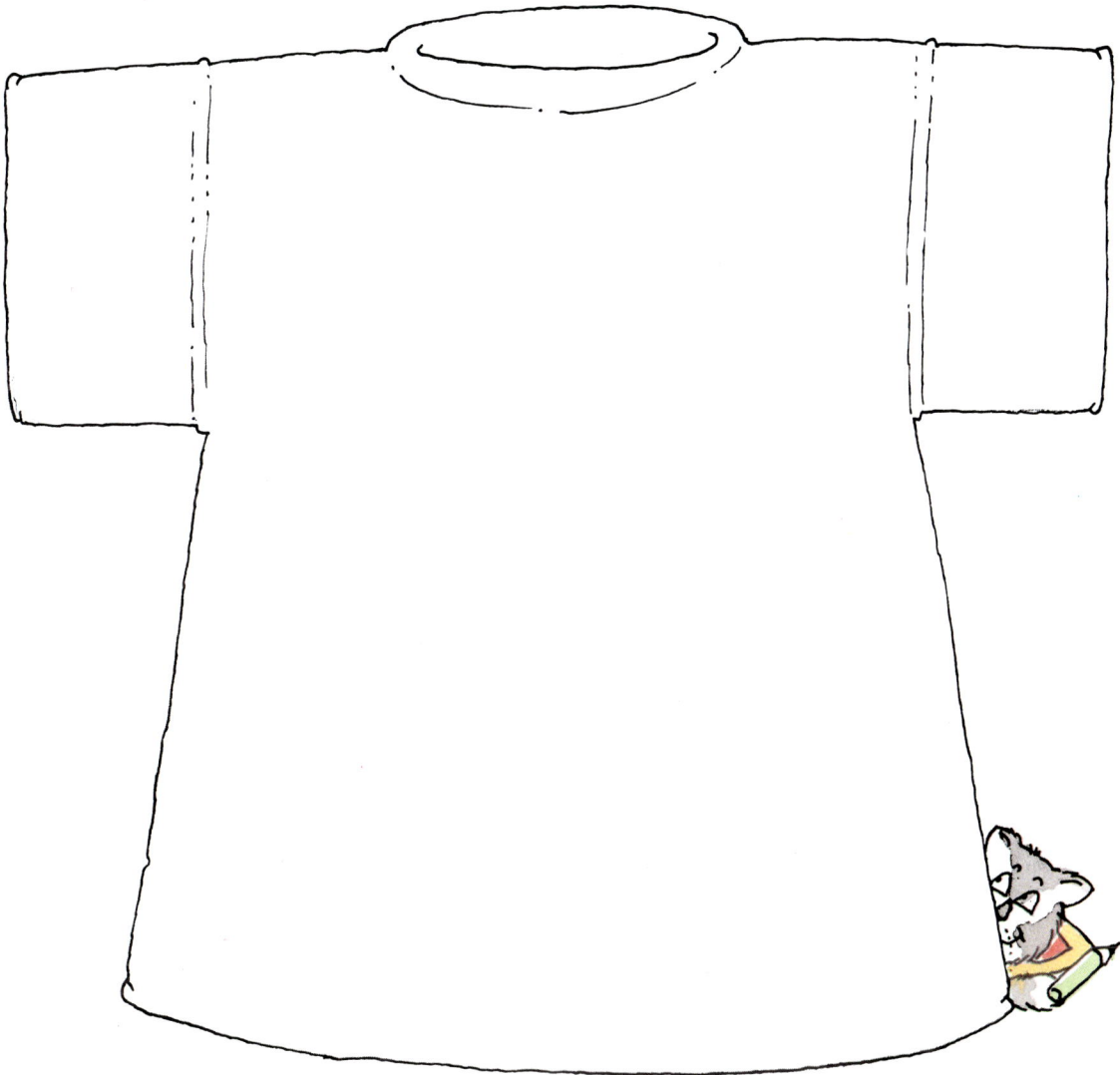

FIND SOMETHING YOU CAN SEE IN A GARDEN.

1 SING A SONG.

I like to fly in the sky,
And see what I can see.
Rivers and mountains,
 cities and clouds,
 I see what I can see.

I like to sit in my chair,
And see what I can see.
Rivers and mountains,
 cities and clouds,
They're all on the TV.

2 LOOK AND FIND.

garden   street   house   school   kitchen   shop   zoo

3 PLAY A GAME.

4 DO A PUZZLE.

Clues

1 You can find this in your schoolbag.
2 You can see this in a zoo.
3 You can eat this in a café.
4 You can see this in your classroom.
5 You can see this in a street.

5 DRAW.

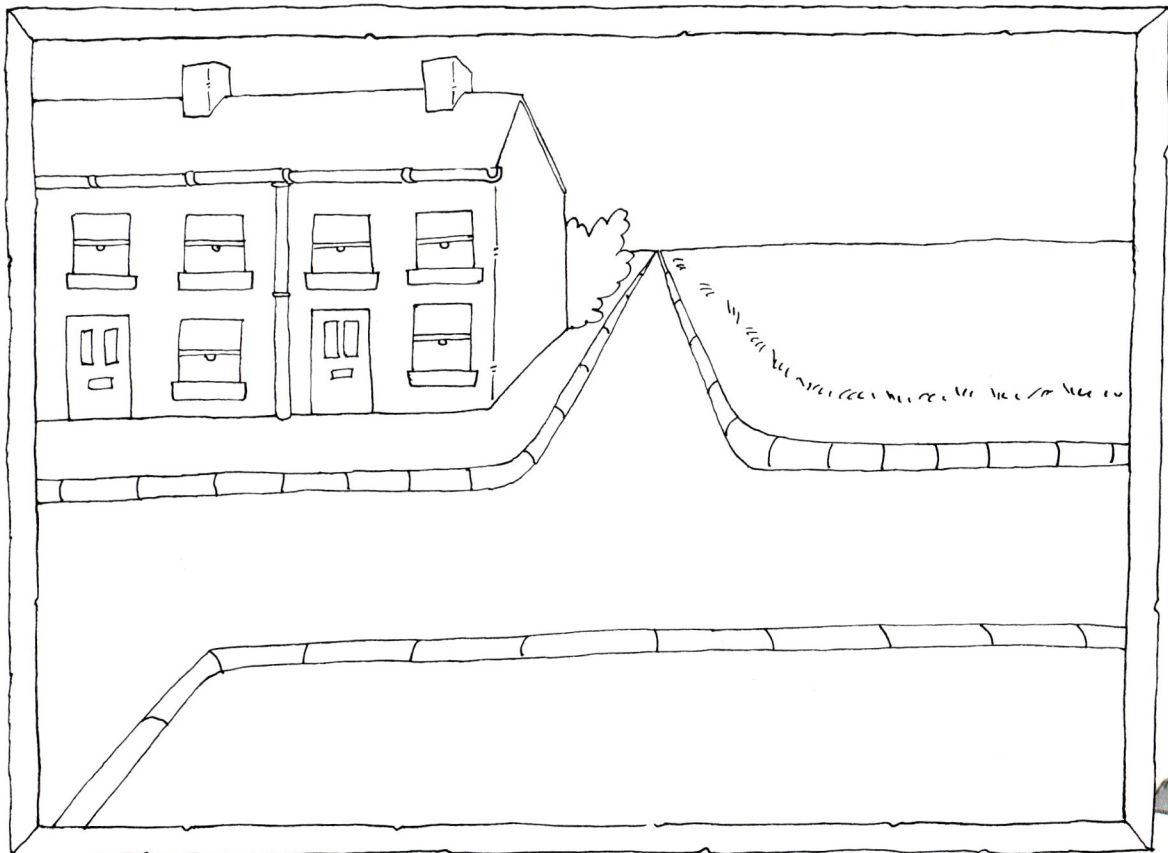

IT'S MONDAY.

1 READ AND LISTEN.

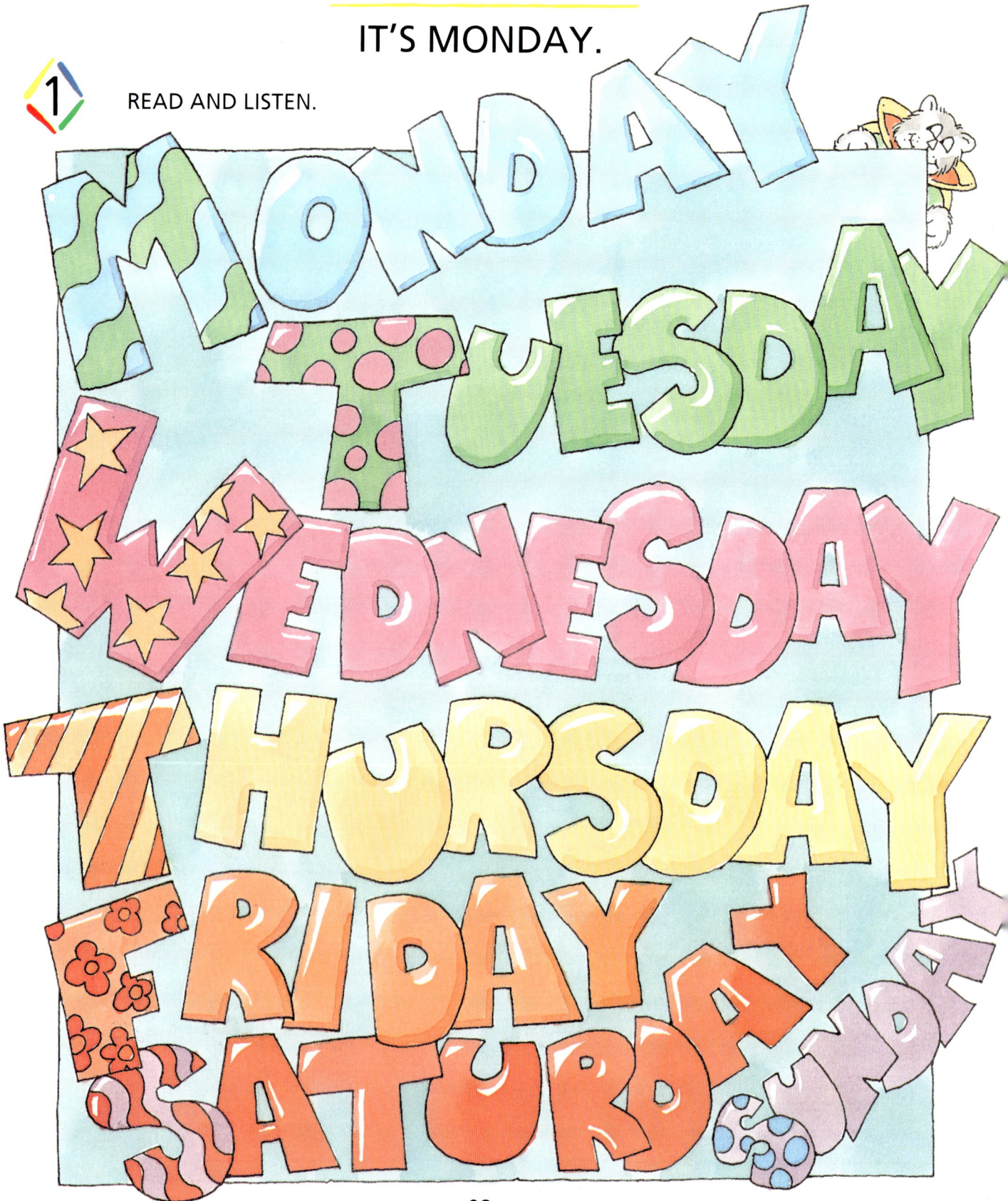

MONDAY

TUESDAY

WEDNESDAY

THURSDAY

FRIDAY

SATURDAY

SUNDAY

2 LISTEN AND FIND.

Draw a line between the pictures and the days.

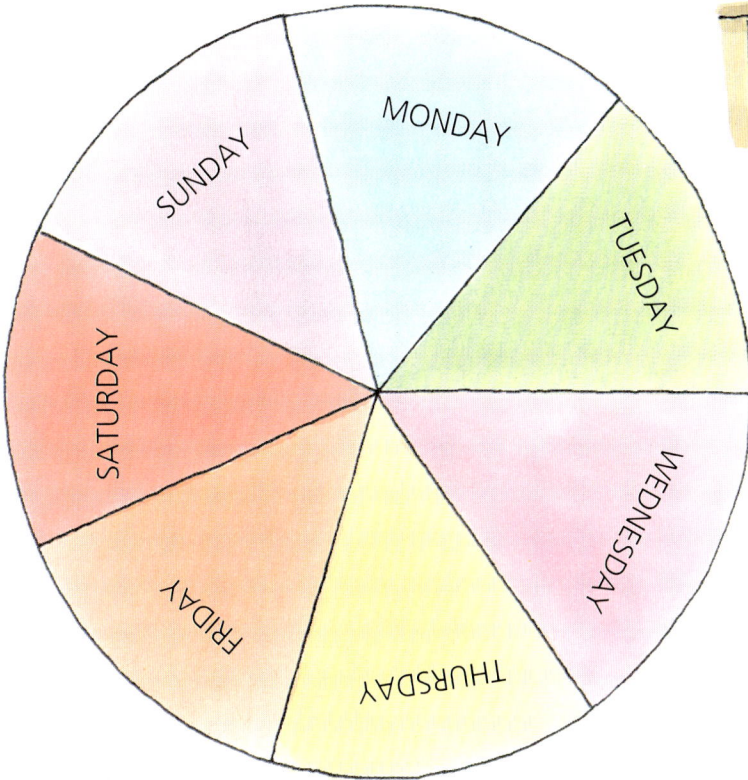

3 LISTEN AND REPEAT.

4 LISTEN AND WRITE.

It's Sunday. Mark is at _____ .

It's Monday. Mark _____ at _____

It's Tuesday morning. Mother is at

the _____ .

CHURCH

SCHOOL

5 LISTEN.

The Days.

SUPERMARKET

6 SING THE SONG.

WHERE'S MY JUMPER?

1 LISTEN AND FIND.

2 LOOK AND SPEAK.

Help Mark find his things.

1 MARK: Oh dear! Where's my T-shirt?
    YOU: Which one?
  MARK: The blue one.
    YOU: It's there — on the bed.

START →

"Can I have a
...... please?"

"Which one?"

"The 🍎 one"

Trace

Cut

Write

Tony

THIS KITCHEN'S A MESS.

1 LISTEN AND FIND.

2 LOOK AND FIND.

clean
dirty
old
new
fresh
empty
full
open
shut
black
white

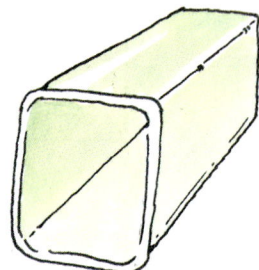

102

3 SPEAK.

	bin kitchen floor ceiling cupboard fish sink bread table mouth	is	dirty. clean. open. shut. old. new. fresh. not fresh. empty. full. disgusting. horrible. nice.
The			
Count Horror's			
His	plates glasses teeth	are	

Count Horror's mouth is open. His teeth are dirty and yellow.

4 ACT IT OUT.

Have some cheese, Boris

Ugh! This cheese is disgusting!

No, it isn't! Shut up and eat it!

THE SAME OR DIFFERENT?

1 LISTEN AND FIND.

2 LOOK AND SAY.   Are these pictures the same or different?

They're the same.   They're different.

3 DO A PUZZLE.   Now look at these pictures. Write 'the same' or 'different'.

1 _____   2 _____   3 _____   4 _____

4 DRAW.   Make these pictures different.

5 PLAY A GAME.

THE TOWN BAND

1 LISTEN AND FIND.

trombones

trumpets

flutes

drums

2 LISTEN AND SAY.

3 LOOK.

In front of the band.
In front of the flutes.
Behind the trumpets.
Behind the flutes.
At the back of the band.

COLOUR THE PICTURE.

4 LISTEN.

THE BAND SONG

5 SING THE SONG.

6 DO A PUZZLE.

Mark is at the front of the class.
Angela is at the back.
Peter is in front of John.

John is in front of Angela.
Susan is behind Mark.
Simon is behind Susan and in front of Peter.

GUESS THE DAY.

1 DO A PUZZLE.

Can you write the days of the week on this puzzle?

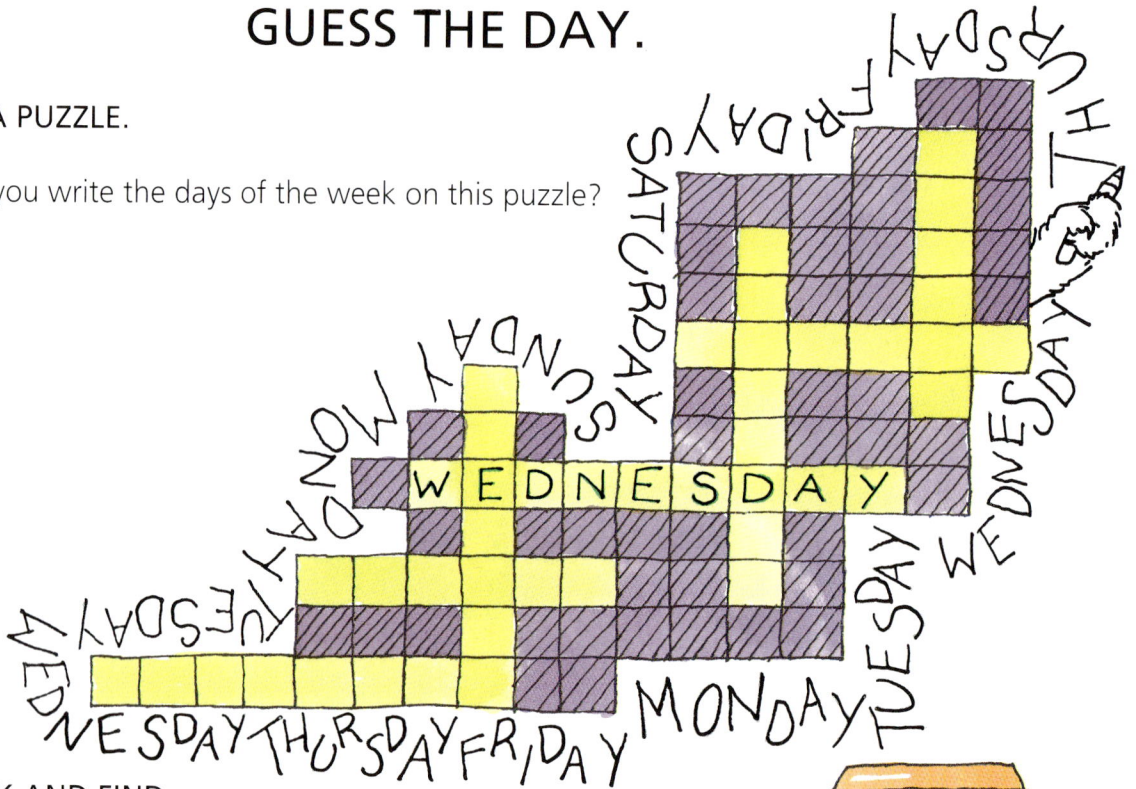

SATURDAY FRIDAY
THURSDAY
SUNDAY MONDAY
WEDNESDAY
WEDNESDAY THURSDAY

W E D N E S D A Y

WEDNESDAY THURSDAY FRIDAY MONDAY TUESDAY

TUESDAY

2 LOOK AND FIND.

1 On Sunday, Mark's bedroom is very tidy.
2 On Monday, it's OK, but his T-shirt is under his bed.
3 On Tuesday, the cupboard is open and the T-shirt is still under the bed.
4 On Wednesday, it's bad. His dirty socks are under the bed, too.

5 On Thursday, it's horrible. His jumper is on the chair and his socks and T-shirt are still under the bed.
6 On Friday, Mark's bag is on the table, and his books are everywhere.
7 On Saturday, it's a terrible mess. His mother is very upset.

3 LISTEN AND WRITE.

Mark! This bedroom's a ....!
Your things are ....!
It's disgusting!
Please ....!

4 PLAY A GAME.

Guess the day!

5 DO A PUZZLE.

BORIS' SOCKS

the green ones

the red ones

COUNT HORROR'S SOCKS

the black ones

NUMBERS

1 LISTEN AND LOOK.

1 2 3 4 5 6 7 8 9 10 11 12 13 14 15 16 17 18 19 20

2 LISTEN AND FIND.

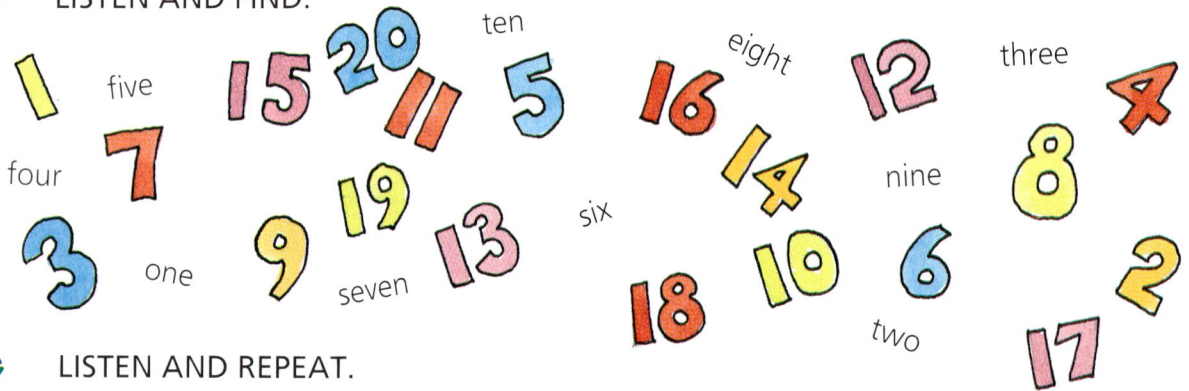

1   five   15 20 11   ten   5   16   eight   12   three   4

four   7   9 19 13   six   14   nine   8

3   one   seven   18   10 6   two   17   2

3 LISTEN AND REPEAT.

4 LISTEN AND DRAW.

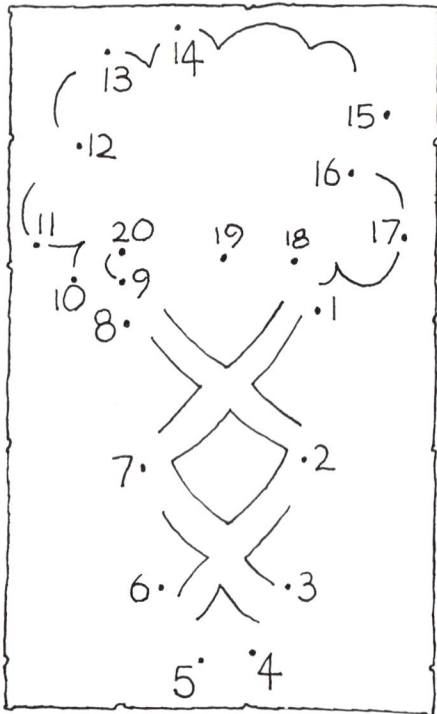

13 14
12   15
16
11 20 19 18 17
10 9
8   1
7   2
6   3
5   4

one

seventeen.   .seven

thirteen.   .nine

eighteen.   two   ten   fifteen   .three

.eight

twenty.   .twelve

fourteen.   .ninete

.four

five   eleven   sixteen

1 What's this? It's an _____

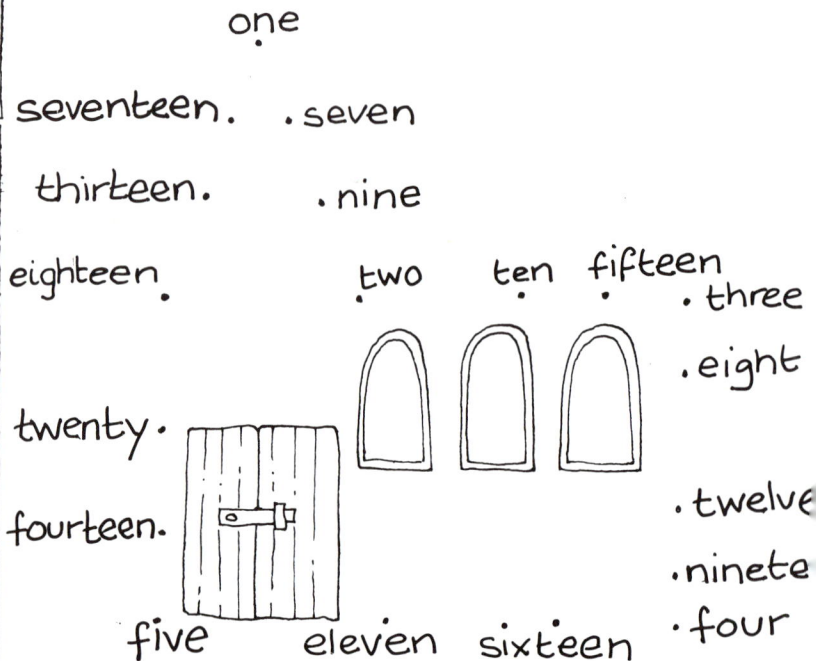

2 What's this? It's a _____

110

5 DO A PUZZLE. What's the difference?

6 LISTEN. The Glasses Song.

SMASH!
CRASH!

7 SING THE SONG.

SS ZZ IZ

8 LISTEN AND FIND.

9 LISTEN AND REPEAT.

TODAY'S MY BIRTHDAY.

1 LISTEN .

2 LISTEN. The Happy Birthday Song.

3 SING THE SONG.

4 WRITE.

Write the words.

Happy _____ to you

_____ Birthday to _____

Happy _____ dear _____

Happy Birthday to you!

5 SPEAK.

How old are you?

I'm 8/9/10

6 PROJECT.

In this class _____ students are 8.

_____ 9.

_____ 10.

7 DRAW A GRAPH.

8 DRAW.

Make a birthday card!

YOU ARE 9 TODAY!   HAPPY BIRTHDAY!

8 TODAY! HOORAY!   HAPPY BIRTHDAY TO YOU!

WHEN'S YOUR BIRTHDAY?

1 LOOK AND LISTEN.

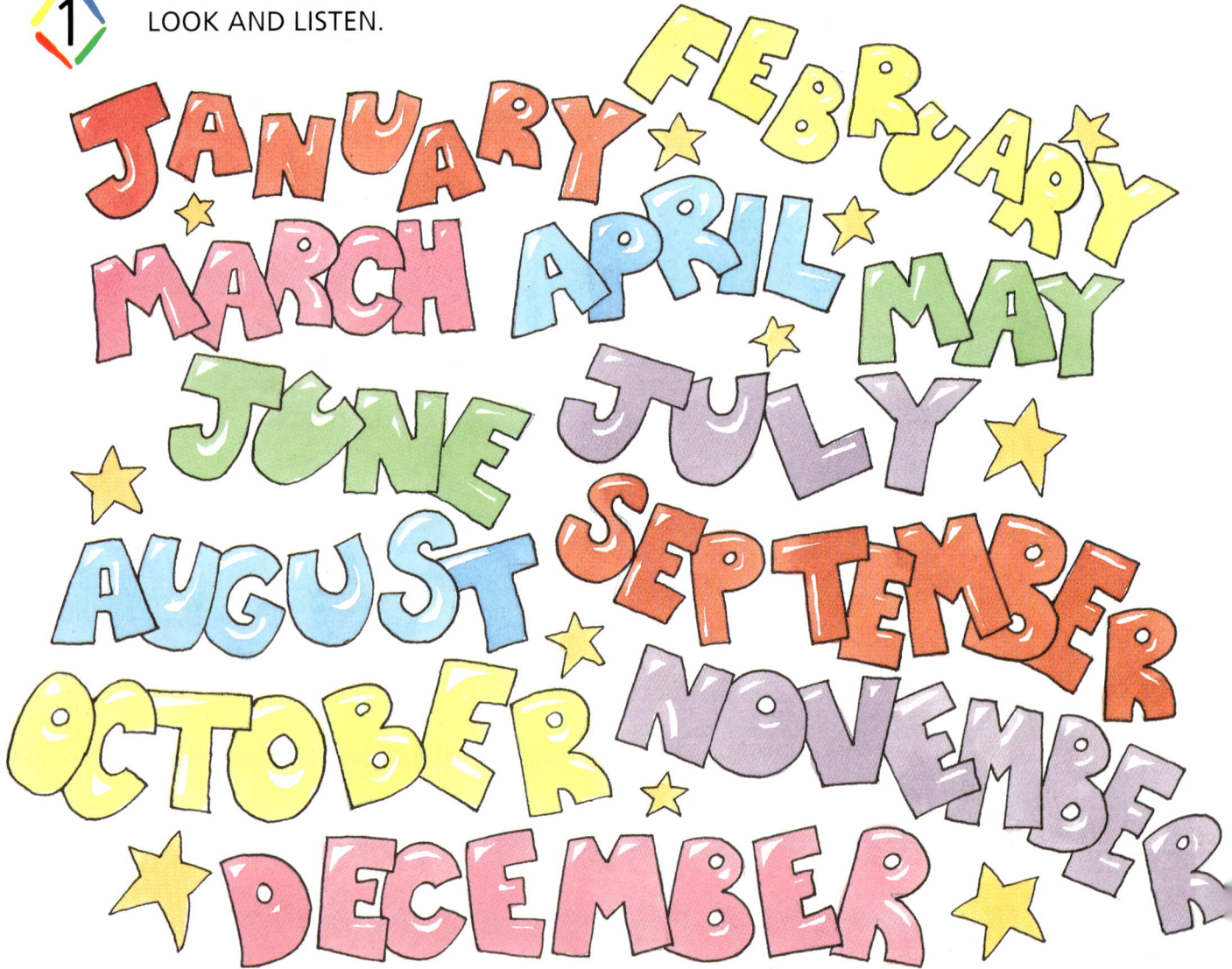

JANUARY FEBRUARY
MARCH APRIL MAY
JUNE JULY
AUGUST SEPTEMBER
OCTOBER NOVEMBER
DECEMBER

2 LISTEN AND REPEAT.

3 LOOK AND FIND.

When's your birthday?

4 WRITE.

My birthday is in _____.

5 PROJECT.

How many children have a birthday in May?

How many children have a birthday in Februar

6 COLOUR THE PICTURES.

JANUARY

APRIL

JULY

DECEMBER

HURRY UP! YOU'RE LATE.

1 LISTEN AND FIND.

2 READ AND FIND.

It's four o'clock.

It's seven o'clock.

It's ten o'clock.

It's twelve o'clock.

It's one o'clock.

It's six o'clock.

3 LISTEN AND REPEAT.

4 COUNT AND SPEAK.

5 LOOK AND SAY.

1

2

3

4

5

6 DRAW.

It's 3 o'clock.

It's 12 o'clock.

It's 7 o'clock.

It's 8 o'clock.

It's 1 o'clock.

7 LISTEN.

8 SPEAK.

IF YOU'RE NUMBER 10, CLAP YOUR HANDS!

1 LISTEN.

2 LISTEN AND REPEAT.

3 LOOK AND FIND.

19 ten   30 eight 17

twenty-six   nineteen

8   seven 7

fifteen   20   twenty-five

10 thirty 15 26

seventeen 25 twenty

4 PLAY A GAME.

NUMBERS 4 AND 10, STAND UP!

PLAY A GAME.

Bingo!

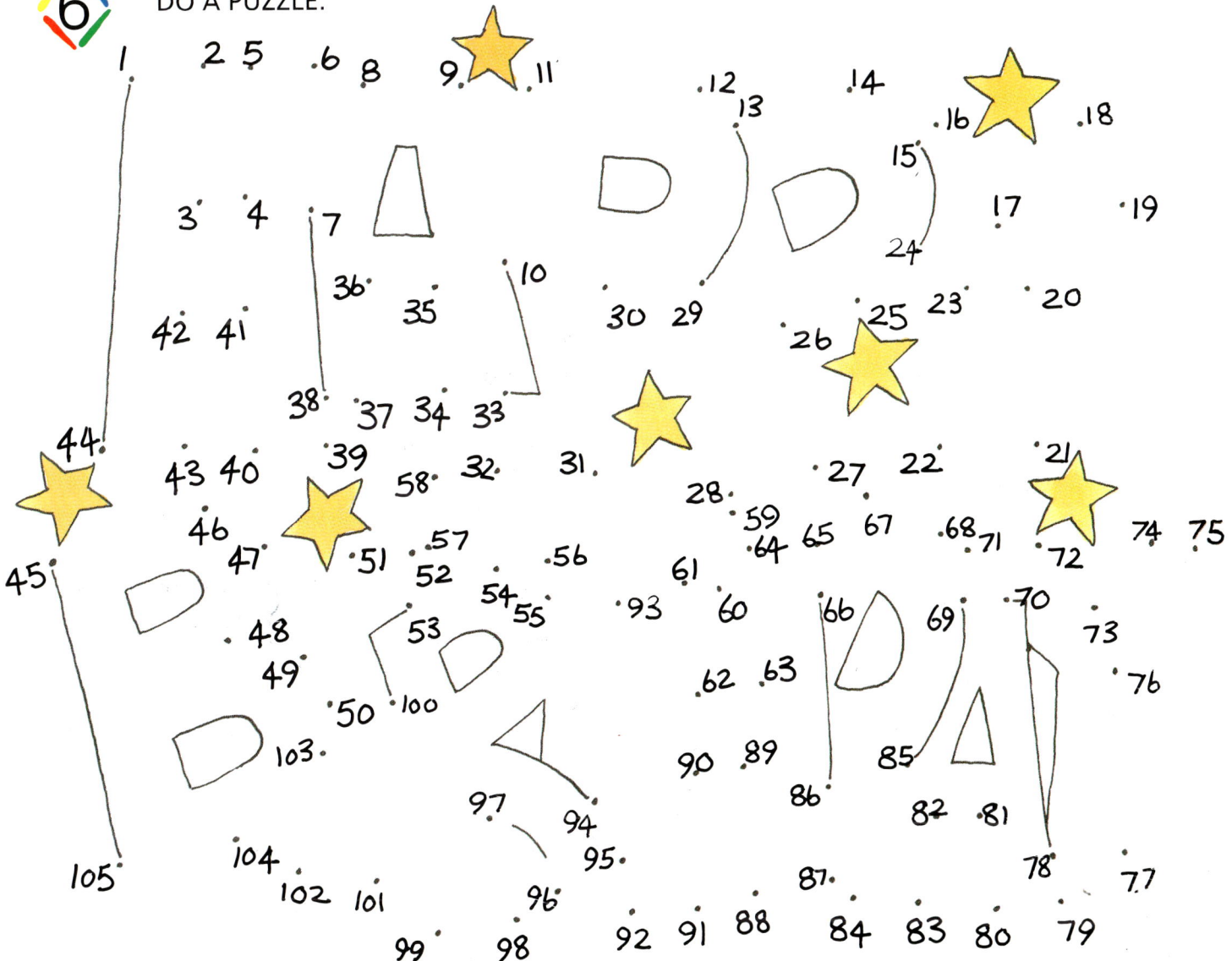

1	12	27	9	26	16	4	23	5	15
29	2	20	30	3	17	24	13	21	14
11	28	10	19	8	18	25	7	6	22

6 DO A PUZZLE.

1 2 5 6 8 9 11 12 13 14 16 18
3 4 7 15 17 19
36 35 10 24
42 41 38 37 34 33 30 29 25 23 20 26
44 43 40 39 58 32 31 27 22 21
46 47 51 52 57 56 28 59 64 65 67 68 71 72 74 75
45 48 53 54 55 93 61 60 66 69 70 73
49 50 100 62 63 76
103 90 89 85 82 81 78 77
97 94 86
104 95 87 79
105 102 101 96 99 98 92 91 88 84 83 80

GOODBYE! LET'S PLAY A GAME.

1 PLAY A GAME.

Everybody start here.

1 If your birthday is in April, May or June, go to 5. If not, go to 7.

2 If you have got something blue on today, go to 9. If not, go to 13.

5 If you are a boy, go to 3. If you are a girl, go to 6.

4 Boys go to 25. Girls go to 26.

3 If you have brown eyes, go to 7. If not, go to 8.

6 If you have one brother, go to 2. If not, go to 10.

7 If you have got grey trousers on today, go to 12. If not, go to 11.

8 If your birthday is in September, October or November, go to 9. If not, go to 14.

9 If you like cheese, go to 15. If not, go to 12.

10 Spell your name and go to 14.

12 If your birthday is in January or March, go to 19. If not, go to 20.

11 Spell your name and go to 14.

13 If you like eggs, go to 15. If you don't like eggs, go to 12.

14 Girls, go to 12. Boys go to 15.

120

22
If you have blue or grey eyes, go to 23. If not, go to 21.

23
If you have got something green on today, go to 24. If not, go to 21.

21
Go to 4! (sorry!)

24
Go to 4! (sorry!)

20
If today is Wednesday or Thursday, go to 18. If not, go to 23.

26
If you live in a house, go to 28. If you live in a flat, go to 29.

25
If you live in a house, go to 28. If you live in a flat, go to 29.

19
If today is Monday or Friday, go to 22. If not, go to 21.

27
Go to 30.

28
Go to 16! (sorry!)

18
If you can play the piano, go to 22. If not, go to 21.

29
Go to 16! (sorry!)

30
OK. Go to the Finish!

17
If you can swim, go to 23. If not, go to 22.

FINISH

2 **LISTEN.** The Goodbye Song

16
Go to 27.

15
If you have a dog or a cat, go to 20. If not, go to 19.

WORDLIST

The Wordlist gives all the new words encountered at this level, with reference to the unit and lesson in which they first appear. Vocabulary is frequently recycled in the Pupil's Books and Workbooks. The Wordlist is perhaps longer than that of some other children's courses, but this was a deliberate decision. We believe that it is communicatively effective to equip a child with a large vocabulary, with relatively few structures and with the confidence and flexibility to use that vocabulary within the structures that he or she knows.

A

a (1.2)
absurd (8.4)
act (*v*) (1.4)
afraid (7.4)
Africa (8.2)
again (2.1)
all (6.3)
am (*v*) (1.2)
an (4.6)
animal (4.4)
apple (5.1)
apple pie (5.2)
April (10.3)
are (*v*) (1.3)
around (7.6)
as (7.6)
at once (7.4)
at the back (9.5)
at the front (9.5)
August (10.3)
Australia (8.2)

B

bad (9.6)
badge (1.2)
bag (7.2)
ball (3.3)
banana (4.1)
band (9.5)
bar (1.1)
bath (2.2)
bathroom (2.2)
be (7.4)
beans (5.2)
beautiful (6.3)
bed (2.2)
bedroom (2.2)
bee (3.5)
beginning (6.2)
behind (9.5)
be sick (*v*) (5.6)
between (9.1)
bin (9.3)
bird (3.4)
birthday (10.2)
biscuit (5.2)
black (4.1)
blouse (7.1)
board (7.3)
book (4.1)
boy (1.2)
branch (7.6)

bread (5.3)
brother (8.2)
brown (4.3)
bus (1.1)
but (8.4)

C

cabbage (4.5)
cafe (8.6)
can (*v*) (4.3)
can't (*v*) (7.5)
car (2.3)
careful (7.4)
carrot (4.5)
castle (2.1)
cat (1.3)
catch (*v*) (3.3)
ceiling (9.3)
chair (2.1)
chart (6.3)
cheap (8.5)
cheese (5.3)
chicken (4.4)
China (8.2)
chip (5.2)
church (9.1)
cinema (1.1)
city (8.6)
clap (*v*) (1.3)
class (7.3)
classroom (7.3)
clean (9.3)
clock (2.5)
clothes (7.1)
cloud (8.6)
cold (1.1)
colour (*v*) and (*n*) (1.2)
come in (*v*) (2.1)
come on (*v*) (1.4)
come out (*v*) (7.4)
comic (7.2)
copy (*v*) (6.4)
cow (2.3)
crash (10.1)
cry (*v*) (8.4)
cupboard (7.3)
cut (*v*) (1.2)

D

Daddy (1.4)
dance (*v*) (8.4)
day (9.1)
December (10.3)

describe (*v*) (7.1)
desk (7.3)
difference (10.1)
different (9.4)
dinner (5.2)
dirty (9.3)
disgusting (9.3)
do (*v*) (1.4)
dog (2.3)
don't (*v*) (5.3)
door (2.1)
draw (*v*) (2.1)
dress (7.1)
drink (1.1)
drum (2.5)
duck (4.4)

E

ear (6.4)
egg (5.4)
eight (2.1)
eighteen (10.1)
elastic (6.4)
elephant (5.4)
eleven (10.1)
empty (9.3)
England (8.1)
English (1.1)
everybody (3.4)
everywhere (4.1)
eye (6.3)

F

face (6.4)
fair (6.6)
falling down (*v*) (4.3)
farm (2.3)
fat (6.6)
father (8.2)
favourite (4.2)
February (10.3)
fifteen (10.1)
find (*v*) (1.1)
finish (10.6)
first (3.2)
fish (5.2)
five (2.1)
flat (2.1)
floor (9.3)
flower (2.4)
flute (2.5)
fly (*v*) (8.4)
fold (*v*) (1.6)

food (5.1)
for (5.1)
four (2.1)
fourteen (10.1)
France (8.1)
French (8.1)
fresh (9.3)
Friday (9.1)
fridge (2.2)
friend (7.1)
from (8.1)
fruit (4.5)
full (9.3)

G

game (1.3)
garden (1.4)
German (8.1)
Germany (8.1)
girl (1.2)
give (*v*) (5.6)
glass (9.3)
glue (*v*) (1.3)
go (*v*) (10.6)
go away (*v*) (3.2)
good (1.5)
good afternoon (3.1)
goodbye (1.4)
good evening (3.1)
good morning (3.1)
grape (4.5)
graph (10.2)
Greece (8.1)
Greek (8.1)
green (4.1)
grey (4.2)
grow (*v*) (7.6)
guess (*v*) (3.2)

H

hair (6.4)
hall (2.1)
hamburger (1.1)
happy (9.1)
has (*v*) (4.6)
have (*v*) (5.1)
have (got) (6.5)
he (7.1)
hello (I.W)
her (7.3)
his (6.4)
hole (6.4)
holiday (10.6)
hooray (3.2)
horrible (5.2)
horse (4.4)
hot (1.1)
house (2.1)
How are you? (1.3)
How many? (4.3)
How old? (10.2)
hungry (5.5)
hurry (*v*) (1.4)

I

I (1.2)
ice cream (1.1)
if (6.3)
in (7.6)
India (8.2)
in front of (9.5)
is (*v*) (1.4)
it (1.4)
Italian (8.1)
Italy (8.1)

J

January (10.3)
July (10.3)
jumper (6.2)
June (10.3)

K

kangaroo (8.2)
kind (6.3)
kitchen (2.2)
knife (7.2)
know (*v*) (7.5)

L

late (10.4)
leader (9.5)
leaf (7.6)
lemon (4.5)
lemonade (5.5)
let's (*v*) (3.2)
like (*v*) (5.3)
line (9.1)
listen (*v*) (1.1)
live (*v*) (8.2)
llama (5.1)
London (8.1)
long (6.6)
look (*v*) (1.1)
look at (*v*) (3.2)
lovely (5.2)

M

magic (1.6)
make (*v*) (1.2)
March (10.3)
market (5.6)
mask (6.4)
May (10.3)
me (3.2)
meat (5.3)
mess (9.2)
milk (5.5)
Monday (9.1)
monkey (5.1)
mother (8.2)
mountain (8.6)
mouse (6.3)
mouth (6.4)

much (5.1)
Mummy (1.4)
my (2.1)

N

name (3.2)
nest (7.6)
new (4.2)
next (3.1)
nine (3.3)
nineteen (10.1)
no (3.1)
noise (4.6)
nose (6.4)
not (3.4)
nothing (8.3)
November (10.3)
now (1.5)
number (3.2)

O

o'clock (10.4)
October (10.3)
of course (5.1)
Oh dear! (3.3)
OK (3.2)
old (9.3)
one (2.1)
onion (5.2)
only (8.3)
open (*v*) (9.3)
orange (4.2)
out (1.4)

P

panda (8.2)
paper (6.4)
Paris (8.1)
pasta (5.3)
pear (4.5)
pen (7.2)
pencil (7.2)
penguin (8.4)
piano (10.6)
picture (2.4)
pig (4.4)
pink (4.2)
pizza (1.1)
plane (3.4)
plate (9.3)
play (*v*) (1.3)
please (3.6)
Portugal (8.1)
Portuguese (8.1)
potato (4.5)
practise (*v*) (3.6)
project (10.3)
pull (*v*) (4.3)
puppet (1.3)
purple (4.2)
put (*v*) (6.4)
puzzle (1.4)

Q

queen (6.2)
quiet (7.4)

R

rabbit (5.1)
rainbow (4.2)
rat (8.2)
read (v) (2.2)
ready (3.2)
really (8.5)
red (4.1)
register (7.4)
remember (v) (6.4)
repeat (v) (3.1)
restaurant (2.3)
rhyme (3.2)
rice (5.2)
right (8.3)
river (8.6)
robot (3.2)
roll (v) (4.3)
rubber (7.2)
ruler (7.2)

S

said (v) (5.6)
salad (5.2)
same (9.4)
sandwich (1.1)
Saturday (9.1)
say (v) (3.1)
schoolbag (8.6)
see (v) (4.3)
September (10.3)
seven (2.1)
seventeen (10.1)
she (7.1)
sheep (2.3)
shirt (7.1)
shoe (7.1)
short (6.6)
show (v) (7.3)
shut (v) (9.3)
shut up (v) (9.3)
sick (5.6)
silly (7.4)
sing (v) (1.3)
sink (7.5)
sister (8.2)
sit down (v) (2.1)
sitting room (2.1)
six (2.1)
sixteen (10.1)
skirt (7.1)
sky (4.1)
sleep (v) (8.3)
smash (10.1)
snack (1.1)
snake (1.3)
so (1.5)
sock (7.1)
sofa (2.2)
some (4.5)

something (6.2)
song (I.W)
sorry (7.4)
soup (1.6)
Spain (8.1)
Spanish (8.1)
speak (v) (1.2)
special (10.2)
spell (v) (6.2)
stand up (v) (3.2)
star (1.1)
start (v) (7.4)
steak (5.2)
stick (v) (1.2)
still (9.6)
stir (v) (6.5)
stop (v) (1.1)
street (2.3)
student (6.3)
Sunday (9.1)
Superman (3.4)
supermarket (1.1)
swim (v) (10.6)
Swiss (8.1)
Switzerland (8.1)

T

table (2.2)
take (v) (7.4)
tall (6.6)
taxi (1.1)
teacher (1.4)
teeth (6.4)
ten (3.3)
terrible (4.6)
thank you (3.2)
That's wrong! (3.3)
them (6.4)
then (5,2)
there (4.6)
these (6.4)
they (6.3)
thin (6.6)
thing (8.3)
thirsty (5.5)
thirteen (10.1)
thirty (10.5)
this (2.1)
those (8.5)
three (2.1)
throw (v) (3.3)
Thursday (9.1)
tie (7.1)
tiger (2.3)
today (7.4)
toilet (2.2)
tomato (5.1)
tomorrow (9.1)
tooth (6.4)
town (9.5)
trace (v) (1.2)
Transylvania (8.2)
tree (2.4)
trombone (9.5)
trousers (7.1)

trumpet (9.5)
T-shirt (7.1)
Tuesday (9.1)
turkey (4.4)
turn round (v) (3.2)
TV (2.2)
twelve (10.1)
twenty (10.1)
twenty-eight (10.5)
twenty-five (10.5)
twenty-four (10.5)
twenty-nine (10.5)
twenty-one ((10.5)
twenty-seven (10.5)
twenty-six (10.5)
twenty-three (10.5)
twenty-two (10.5)
twin (1.5)
two (2.1)

U

umbrella (5.4)
under (8.3)
upset (9.6)

V

vampire (6.6)
vegetables (4.5)
very (3.4)
violin (6.2)

W

want (v) (8.5)
was (v) (5.6)
water (5.5)
we (6.5)
Wednesday (9.1)
weekend (9.1)
welcome (v) (I.W)
went (v) (5.6)
what (1.6)
What's the matter? (8.3)
where (7.5)
where from? (8.1)
which (8.5)
white (4.1)
who (1.5)
why (8.4)
window (7.3)
with (4.6)
wood (7.6)
wool (6.4)
write (v) (3.2)

Y

year (10.6)
yellow (4.1)
yes (3.1)
you (1.3)
your (1.5)

Z

zebra (8.2)
zoo (2.3)